D0070529

ADVENTISM
THE SECOND COMING OF CHRIST

Books by

WILLIAM P. KING

As Author

THE PRACTICE OF THE PRINCIPLES OF JESUS
FAITH IN THE DIVINE FATHERHOOD
RIGHT AND WRONG IN AN AGE OF CONFUSION
ADVENTISM

As Editor

BEHAVIORISM: A Battle Line
HUMANISM: Another Battle Line
SOCIAL PROGRESS AND CHRISTIAN IDEALS

ADVENTISM

The
Second Coming of Christ

By
WILLIAM P. KING, 1871—

With an Introduction by
HALFORD E. LUCCOCK

3063780

ABINGDON-COKESBURY PRESS
NEW YORK ● *NASHVILLE*

ADVENTISM
COPYRIGHT, MCMXLI
BY WHITMORE & STONE

All rights in this book are reserved. No part of the text may be reproduced in any form without written permission of the publishers, except brief quotations used in connection with reviews in a magazine or newspaper.

PRINTED IN THE UNITED STATES OF AMERICA

To

**THE CHRISTIANS OF ALL CHURCHES WHO
ARE SINCERELY ENDEAVORING TO FIND THE
TRUE MEANING OF THE SACRED SCRIPTURES**

INTRODUCTION

THE SUBJECT OF THIS BOOK HAS BEEN FOR GENERations like the little "buffer state" of Belgium. Over that unhappy land, once again under a conqueror's heel, battles have been fought and refought for centuries, from long before Caesar's invasions down through Waterloo to the present year. So the subject of Adventism, with the clashing of premillennialists and postmillenialists, with many an "alarum and excursion" against those who will not shout the shibboleth of either party, has been a battleground. The very subject has often been a reminder of

"Old, unhappy far-off things
And battles long ago."

But all the battles were not fought long ago. They are still going on. The whole subject, which has such fascination for many minds, has been the cause of much confusion, controversy, and bitterness among many sincere and earnest Christian people. This controversy about when the devil is to be chained up has had this sad effect in many cases, that the devil of strife has been let loose in congregations and the Church. It has caused disastrous

splits in Christian forces when there is desperate
need for the unity of the spirit in the bond of
peace.

To this situation and need Dr. King has brought
both sweetness and light in this little book. It is
as clear as sunlight and breathes a spirit of calm
reasonableness. Dr. King does not lead a charge
of the Light Brigade in this volume. He is not
interested in verbal flayings or any deviltries of de-
bate. He is deeply interested in opening the Scriptures, and seeking, by quiet, frank, and humble ex-
amination of them, what light they throw on the
subject of Adventism. It is difficult for me to
see how any fair-minded reader of this book, who
really finds his seat of authority in the teaching
and spirit of our Lord Jesus Christ, will fail to
realize how deeply based in the Scripture Dr. King's
conclusions are.

Dr. King brings light rather than heat to the
discussion of Adventism. There has been far too
much heat already. There is an old patristic teaching to the effect that the fires of hell give heat but
not light. It can be truly said that wherever we
have heat without light we have not a heavenly
but a diabolical fire.

I have read the book with great profit and enlightenment and am honored in having the opportunity of here recording my appreciation. Every

chapter has caused me to rejoice that the author is not like Lady Britonart in Bernard Shaw's play *Major Barbara*. Mr. Shaw says of that noble lady, that she feels that "her conscience is clear and her duty done when she has called everybody names." Dr. King is not gifted in invectives. His duty is not done in name-calling, but in cogent reasoning based on patient, devoted study of the Scripture.

Another feature of the volume which should commend it to every Christian is its positive quality. For the author's chief interest is not denial of this or that, but affirmation. The positive core of his teaching is a tremendous unshaken faith in the ultimate victory of God. This faith breaks out in the final chapter like the soul-stirring music of a Hallelujah Chorus. He writes, "It is this power of a living, loving God that will win the battle of Armageddon, the final conflict of the Apocalypse. . . . . Ultimate victory is made certain by the moral order of the world and by the omnipotence of the sovereign God."

It would seem ridiculous in me to feel a note of autobiography in this volume which has scarcely a personal reference from start to finish. Yet I do feel it distinctly. For it gives evidence of a life-long study of the Scriptures. This book has been lived before it was written, in the sense that it comes from many years of living with the Word of God. The thoroughness, the tolerance and insight with which it treats all the passages in the Old and New Testaments bearing on the nature of "things to come" is deeply impressive.

I am confident that the book will do a large service in helping people to understand more clearly and to love more deeply "the Christ who is and is to be."

HALFORD E. LUCCOCK

FOREWORD

MANY GOOD PEOPLE HAVE BEEN REPELLED FROM the apocalyptic portion of the Bible, since it has been capitalized by religious fanaticism. A true method of interpretation will result in a higher valuation of apocalyptic literature.

The books of Daniel and Revelation served a necessary function in preserving the religious faith in the dark days of emergency and crisis. It is my purpose in this volume to assist in removing the bizarre and grotesque fancies which have resulted in obscuring this portion of the Scriptures. The effort is made in so far as possible to be nontechnical. However, one cannot avoid such terms as "parousia," "apocalyptic," "apocryphal," "postmillennialism," "premillennialism," and "eschatology." If it becomes necessary for some readers to consult the dictionary, the exercise will not be unprofitable.

I am writing from the slant of no one denomination, but am endeavoring to combat an error which brings hurt to all of the churches. The doctrine has not been more strongly resisted on account of an aversion to religious controversy. In contrast with the abundance of Adventist literature, very few books have been written by representatives of the evangelical churches in refutation of the doctrine. The notion is disproved by all of the standard biblical commentaries, but the laymen do not have access to these volumes. The preachers have not sufficiently felt the responsibility of instructing their membership, some of whom become easy victims of glib quoters of proof texts, who construct marvelous maps of all future ages. It is our obligation and our best opportunity by way of prevention to safeguard the minds of our young people against the errors of Adventism. They should be instructed in the historical method of scriptural interpretation. When people once become possessed of this notion, it becomes an obsession. It is useless to argue, since that which is not based on at least a measure of reason cannot be removed by reason.

I recognize the impossibility in a book of the size of this to do full justice to all of the phases of this controversial question. I can only hope to put readers on the way of finding the true viewpoint. Some will regard the book as too brief for a fair presentation of the subject. Others may have preferred an even more concise statement of the issues involved. But since it is hardly possible to please all, I send the book forth as it is with the hope that it may accomplish the purpose for which it was intended.

I wish to acknowledge my grateful indebtedness to several authors listed in the Bibliography.

Concerning some matters I have not been able to speak with certainty. But as to the distinctive doctrines of Adventism it is very certain that they have no foothold either in reason or revelation.

When a person once becomes possessed of this theory it becomes an obsession, a mania. All the king's horses and all the king's men cannot pull him right again. I have known only a few instances in which persons have been brought back to a sane view of the Scriptures. It is a matter of the most urgent importance that our church people who have not been caught in the toils of this theory shall be rightly instructed. We must see that the young people in our church schools are not victimized by this false teaching. The true procedure is one of prevention, that will safeguard our members against the glib quoters of proof texts, and detached passages of Scripture. My earnest and sincere wish is that this volume may make a helpful contribution to an intelligent Christian faith.

WILLIAM P. KING

CONTENTS

I

THE MAIN ISSUES

WE SHOULD CLEARLY UNDERSTAND THAT THE biblical teaching of the second coming of Christ is not called in question. The theory which I propose to refute has come to be termed "Adventism," which regards the coming as premillennial; that is, as occurring before the thousand-year period mentioned in Revelation 20:4-5. Postmillennialism is the theory that Christ comes after the period of a conflict and victory over Satan.

Adventists fall into the fallacy of holding before their hearers strict premillennialism and strict postmillennialism with the assumption that you must choose one or the other. But between two false notions you are not required to choose either. We find no scriptural foundation for any one thousand years of ideal conditions on earth either before or after the coming of Christ.

The premillennialists believe that the world will grow hopelessly worse before the second advent.

17

The postmillennialists hold that the world will reach an ideal condition before that event. While this is a far more hopeful doctrine, yet it is in error when it attaches any literal significance to a thousand years reign of Christ. If the postmillennialists think that the thousand years represent the period in which we are now living, they overlook the fact that instead of being bound Satan is very evidently loose in the world.

A PHYSICAL REIGN

We recognize the devotion and sincerity of many advocates of Adventism. This makes the error the more deplorable. If it had been the purpose of the Bible to teach a thousand years' physical reign of Christ on earth, it would certainly not have been left out of sixty-five of the books and mentioned in only one book in a symbolical passage which may be variously interpreted. If true, it is impossible to imagine that Jesus would have made no mention of it, nor the writers of the four Gospels nor Paul nor the writers of the other Epistles. To construct a theological system on this sort of foundation is an unscriptural and unreasonable procedure. The doctrine of Adventism is not even good literalism. Interpret the Bible as literally as you please and you find no sufficient basis for this theory. We cannot be positive as to some questions, but we can be positive as to the errors of Adventism.

The incident is related of President Patton that in the classroom he asked a young man to explain the origin of sin. The youth replied in substance that he had known but had forgotten. Dr. Patton replied, "What a pity! The only man who ever knew has forgotten!"

As touching the mistaken views under discussion, we are left in no uncertainty. The fact is so evident that Adventism is without scriptural foundation that I make the promise here and now that I will myself become an ardent convert to this doctrine and proclaim it as I have opportunity if any brother will show me the least intimation in all the teaching of Jesus or the least suspicion of an intimation of any thousand years' physical reign on earth. The only dim shadow of a foundation for the theory consists in a fanciful interpretation of symbolic references in a highly figurative passage of Scripture, chapter twenty of Revelation.

Adventists cling to an idea of Christ's kingdom which was forever refuted by the manner of his incarnation, and has been persistently refuted by all the centuries of Christian life and history. Its survival despite its follies and mistakes is a strange case in which error crushed to earth will rise again. It is especially urgent at this time to fortify the

19

people against this error. I have received letters from many pastors as to the best way to counteract this heresy which has invaded their churches. It has made inroads into practically all of the large Protestant churches, and misleads the uninformed.

The adherents of this view make a violent attack on their opponents as rationalists and mutilators of the Bible, with the assumption that they are set for the defense of the faith. The effect of the notion, however, if generally prevalent, would be to produce more skepticism than it could possibly cure. For the Church to set forth as a necessary part of the faith the crude and mechanical notions of Adventism would drive the educated minds of our modern age into infidelity. But there must be the heartiest Christian welcome of those holding various opinions into the fellowship of the Church. The Christian Church must be all-inclusive of those who are sincerely devoted to Jesus Christ. This is not to prevent a resistance to erroneous views and the advocacy of the sane spiritual viewpoint. The main issue is between a true and a false understanding of the Scriptures.

According to Hastings' *Dictionary of the Bible,* "The idea of a millennial reign of the Messiah on earth is found in Jewish apocalypse but there is no authority for it in the teachings of our Lord. It seems difficult to attach to it any meaning of per-

manent spiritual value; moreover, in its materialistic forms it has been a source of weakness rather
than strength to Christian eschatology." It has
produced fanatical expectations and date-fixings
through the centuries.

THE FUNCTION OF PROPHECY

In addition to the idea of a millennial kingdom,
another major issue is the Adventist perversion of
prophecy. This will be brought out more fully in
the chapter on "The Nature of Prophecy." Both
in *Beacon Lights of Prophecy,* by W. A. Spicer,
and in the *Scofield Reference Bible* the entire future
history of the world is seen to be portrayed by the
prophets and apocalyptists. At the hands of these
two prognosticators the Bible becomes a medley
and a jumble of flighty speculations. This is not to
question their sincerity. I am convinced that the
writers are self-deluded and are not intentional
deluders of others. Practically all biblical scholars
recognize that the prophets dealt largely with their
present and the immediate future.

II

ZEAL NOT ACCORDING TO
KNOWLEDGE

IT IS NOT POSSIBLE TO DWELL AT LENGTH ON THE various sects who hold to the premillennial idea. The different groups inclusive of those bearing the Adventist name would reach a total of one million members. When there is added to these the premillennialists who retain their membership in the large denominations, the total would possibly reach three millions.

THE BELIEF IN CHILIASM

With varying viewpoints on minor matters all Adventists hold the doctrine of the physical reign of Christ on earth for a thousand years. We can consider only this central feature held by all of the sects.

Some six groups bear the name of Adventists: Evangelical Adventists; Advent Christians; Seventh-Day Adventists; Church of God, closely al-

22

lied with the Seventh-Day Adventists; The Life and Advent Union; and Church of God in Christ Jesus, or Age-to-Come Adventists. Dr. Elmer T. Clark, in a volume *The Small Sects in America,* shows that they are for the most part millenarian. The Pentecostal and Perfectionist sects, that broke off from The Methodist Church; the Christian and Missionary Alliance, founded by A. B. Simpson, who withdrew from the Presbyterian Church; the Catholic Apostolic Church, or the "Irvingites"; the International Church of the Foursquare Gospel, sponsored by Aimee Semple McPherson; the Christian Catholic Church of John Alexander Dowie; the Plymouth Brethren; the Mennonites; and numerous smaller groups are all Adventists. These sects spring out of conditions of poverty, but a number of financially prosperous people are attracted to the doctrine. Mention may be made also of Mormonism, whose creed is thus stated: "We believe in the literal gathering of Israel and in the restoration of the ten tribes; that Zion will be built on this continent; that Christ will reign visibly upon the earth, and that the earth will be renewed and receive its paradisaic glory." The Mormons place the seat of this empire in Jackson County, Missouri. We are sure that this millennial reign is as likely to be in Missouri as in Jerusalem.

The Russellites, the followers of Pastor Russell,

23

are termed also International Bible Students' Association, or Jehovah's Witnesses, and are the most aggressive. Judge J. F. Rutherford is the successor of Pastor Russell. Their literature is circulated with the most intense activity. *The Divine Plan of the Ages* has been translated into thirty-five languages. A cruel and unjust persecution has been inflicted on this group. They have conscientious scruples against saluting the flag as a violation of the Second Commandment. The Supreme Court ruled that compulsory flag saluting is constitutional and that children may be barred from public schools for refusing to do so. As a matter of fact, enlightenment is the only cure, and to shut the children off from educational opportunities is extremely unfortunate.

The Seventh-Day Adventists are the largest group, numbering 143,000. They publish more than two hundred periodicals. As is well known, they have established sanitariums, the influence of which should not be discounted. They far surpass in their expenditure for foreign and evangelistic work the larger Protestant churches in proportion to their numbers. The zeal of Adventists is to be commended, even though in the realm of religious doctrine it is without knowledge.

AN INTELLIGENT CHRISTIAN FAITH

We are commanded to love God with our minds. Even if a little learning is a dangerous thing, it is not so dangerous as the same amount of ignorance. We have the old story of a New England fisherman who had been soundly converted in a revival meeting. He became a lay preacher and preached a sermon from the words, "Thou knowest I am an oysterman." When he was informed that the scripture was, "Thou knowest I am an austere man," he replied, "Well, I don't care; I got six converts anyway."

Some good results that may follow in the wake of Adventism do not make reparation for the harm that results from a wrong interpretation of the Scriptures. This conception with its burden of obsolete vagaries is too heavy for the Christian Church to carry. It is impossible to a fully enlightened Christian intelligence. I do not question the sincerity of these leaders. The fact is, their very cocksureness and sincerity make them the more hopeless.

ACTIVE PROPAGANDA

The literature of Adventism is widely disseminated. *Jesus Is Coming,* by W. E. B., has been translated into twenty-five languages, with an enormous sale; and with his juggling of letters and

25

figures, he works havoc among a large number of people. An active propaganda is carried on in support of the literalistic and fantastic interpretation of the Scriptures. No religious propaganda was ever more generously financed. The free distribution of books, tracts, and periodicals indicates that huge sums of money are being spent to further the vagaries of premillennialism. The skill of the late Dr. J. M. Gray of the Moody Bible Institute in making some Hebrew word mean Russia is a marvel to the uninformed. Gog, Magog, and Armageddon all testify that these are the last times, and Mussolini or Hitler is the beast of Revelation. The *Scofield Reference Bible* says that the mention of Rosh, Meshech in Ezekiel 38:2, 3 means Russia, Moscow. The first readers of Ezekiel could not possibly understand what Ezekiel was talking about. One wonders why Ezekiel was so concerned about the generation which was to read the *Scofield Bible* and so little concerned with his contemporaries.

Adventism receives fresh impetus in periods of depression, discouragement, and despair. It thrives on social disorders and confusion, and finds a hotbed for growth in wars and rumors of wars. From century to century Adventism has found the same indications of the "last days." A religious editor recently stated that "among conditions that fit in with prophetic characterization of the end times, are violence in all the earth, the return of the Jews to Palestine, the revival of the Roman Empire, distress of nations unprecedented, and a great apostasy from faith."

The wars now raging in Europe and Asia are producing the same sort of forecasting as marked the World War. In 1917 a declaration signed by Dr. G. Campbell Morgan and other noted churchmen contained the following statements: "The present crisis points toward the close of the times of the Gentiles"; "All human schemes of reconstruction must be subsidiary to the second coming of our Lord." In the distress and desolation that has come to England an English church periodical states that there is a renewal of the doctrine of Adventism.

THE EXPLANATION OF ITS APPEAL

The very goodness of some people mistakenly leads them into Adventism. Their antagonism to the evil forces which appear to be invulnerably entrenched and their desire for victory lead them to transform Jesus into a supreme military dictator. The apocalyptic viewpoint has been the recourse of many earnest souls as they looked out upon the strong evil forces of the world. God must intervene in a direct, visible way or all is lost. The apocalyptic literature of Daniel and Revelation kept hope alive when wickedness was on the throne.

There has come the perversion of that which served a good purpose in its day. To some modern religionists the Book of Revelation suggests only speculations concerning the figure 666 and the thousand years.

Again a forceful appeal is made by Adventists, due to a definite faith in a personal and living God, who is the Almighty in his power. Their view of the divine methods is mistaken, but their unswerving faith in God has a carrying power when in some intellectual circles God is being reduced to the impotence of an impersonal abstraction. The appeal is stronger than a cold rationalism,

"Which weighs out every grain of that which was miraculous before
And sneers the heart down with the scoffing brain."

Adventism protests against a mechanical notion of the world, an automatic human figure with the divine left out. This protest is praiseworthy.

A further popular response is won by an inerrant and mechanical idea of inspiration. The belief in the verbal dictation theory gives to the Adventists such dogmatic cocksureness. They recall to mind the pompous brother who said that he made a mistake only one time and that was when he thought he was mistaken.

A POSITIVE AND VITAL NOTE

Adventism can never be successfully refuted by a mere negative procedure. Over against its pessimism we must proclaim a positive message of God's power and saving grace with hope and spiritual expectancy which is the missing note of both a skeptical liberalism and a superficial literalism.

The only way to meet the deepest need of the human heart at all times—and especially in times of great calamity, when the catastrophic idea catches the popular imagination—is to proclaim a gospel so full of vitality and assurance and power that men will no longer feel the need of a spectacular and dramatic manifestation of miraculous power. Jesus sought to make it clear that in his spiritual personality he would never be absent from the world: "I will not leave you desolate; I come to you"; and "If any man love me he will keep my word; and my Father will love him, and we will come unto him, and make our abode with him." "I am with you all the days even to the end of the world."

It is very true that some consecrated revivalists have been premillennialists, but their success was through the proclamation of the saving power of the gospel and not by their belief in the immediacy of a military millennium. Our supreme need is a spiritual revival which will shame the skepticism of scorners and which will lift the Church out of its complacency. We need to experience the spiritual power which will put heart and faith into our churches, and which will bring to us the apostolic courage before which the cowardly forces of evil, whether in low or high places, are not able to stand. With confident faith and invincible hope we are to be workers together with God in building his kingdom on earth. We are to pray for and expect the continual coming of Christ throughout the far-flung frontiers of the Christian Church. As the Church prays for his personal and spiritual presence, we have the assurance that he will come in an increasing manifestation of power until his final victorious triumph.

A SANE AND VITAL GOSPEL IN NEGLECTED AREAS

It must be confessed with humiliation that the large bodies of Protestantism have failed to minister to the spiritual needs of people who live in manufacturing centers and certain rural sections. These people are left to respond to the only religious appeal that comes to them. The evangelists of Adventism and advocates of other fantastic religious notions find in these neglected areas a fertile soil for the seeds of fanaticism. It is a sin against God and a sin against humanity for the large Protestant churches to neglect the poor and the ignorant. At last we get nowhere with the negative method of exposing the absurdities of the doctrine. If we are to follow the high example of the early Christian Church, our evangelical church must preach the gospel to the poor. The call and the need are urgent. To heed the call and to respond to the need would not only bring an intelligent Christian faith to these people who have been neglected, but would result in the reflex influence of an increased spiritual life and power to the evangelizing churches. In doing this we not only save those to whom we minister from the peril of wild excesses of fanaticism but save ourselves from the peril of a lifeless religious formalism. As we exercise a zeal according to knowledge, then we will have no room in the religious world for that zeal that is not according to knowledge.

III

FACING THE FACTS FAIRLY

IN ALL OF OUR INTERPRETATION, OUR EFFORT should not be to bend the Scripture to fit some pet theory. We should seek to be in accord with the spirit of Christ who came "to bear witness to the truth."

THE SECOND ADVENT IN THE NEW TESTAMENT

The imminence of the second advent permeates the New Testament from the Gospel of Mark to that of John, from the epistles of Paul to Revelation, from the first to the last of the Acts of the Apostles. The parousia is not so prominent in the pastoral epistles to Timothy and Titus and in the Epistle of James, but is not entirely ignored in any part of the New Testament. The earliest Christian literature that has to do with the parousia is that of Paul. In the First Epistle to the Thessalonians he twice uses the expression, "We that are alive," in contrast with those who died before the return of Christ. This first letter resulted in a wild fanaticism which the apostle had to counteract. In the Second Epistle to the Thessalonians he endeavors to relieve the excitement by indicating certain events that prevent a speedy return of Jesus, such as an intervening "apostasy," "the man of sin," and a period of "lawlessness."

In his First Epistle to the Corinthians, Paul writes, "We shall not all sleep, but we shall all be changed." While in the later epistles of Paul less emphasis is placed on the immediate appearance of Christ, yet the idea never entirely disappears. He says in the Epistle to the Romans, "The day of the Lord is at hand," and to the Philippians, one of his latest epistles, "The Lord is at hand." Paul is in accord with the general tenor of the New Testament in that the second coming immediately precedes the final judgment. Paul is entirely free from premillennialism and makes no allusion to any earthly reign of Christ for a thousand years.

The teaching of the second advent is too evident to be overlooked, but this is entirely different from a Judaic kingdom on earth. Following the resurrection of Jesus and his appearance to the disciples, Luke in the first chapter of the Acts quotes the apostles as asking, "Will thou at this time restore the kingdom again unto Israel?" Peter in his

First Epistle writes, "But the end of all things is at hand."

In John's Gospel we find that the coming of Jesus is spiritual rather than physical. The parousia has a meaning distinct from this spiritual presence of Jesus. In the final chapter of John's Gospel we have the words of Jesus to Peter, "If I will that he tarry till I come, what is that to thee?" This clearly refers to the second advent.

THE WORDS OF JESUS

As to the immediacy of the second advent we reach a more difficult and debatable issue when we endeavor to find a consistent record of the attitude of Jesus. The three Synoptic Gospels represent Jesus as declaring that his second advent is near at hand. Some four passages may be quoted.

According to Matthew, before sending out the Twelve, Jesus said, "Verily I say unto you, ye shall not have gone over the cities of Israel, till the Son of man be come." The second passage, in Mark, says, "And he said unto them, Verily I say unto you, there be some here of them that stand by, which shall in no wise taste of death, till they see the kingdom of God come with power." It may be added that the first of these passages is rather too specific in view of the declaration of Jesus, "But of that day or that hour, knoweth no one, not even the angels in heaven, neither the Son but the Father." In the third passage, after describing the coming of Jesus in "clouds with great power and glory," Mark says, "Verily I say unto you this generation shall not pass away until all these things be accomplished." The fourth passage is substantially the same in all of the Synoptics. As given in Mark, it is, "And ye shall see the Son of man sitting at the right hand of power, and coming with the clouds of heaven."

The claim is made that Jesus suffered at the hands of his reporters. In the apocalyptic sections of the Synoptic Gospels, there is an evident blending and confusion of the signs preceding Jerusalem's downfall and the signs of the second advent. These two events are not separated in Matthew, and they are obscured in Mark and Luke. It does not appear to be possible to disentangle the reference to the destruction of Jerusalem and the coming of the Christ. In Mark 13:1-23, the reference appears to be to Jerusalem, and in verses 24-27 to the coming of the Son of Man. In Luke 21:20-24 the fall of Jerusalem is forecast, and in verses 25-28 the advent of Christ. In Matthew 24 the two events are blended.

Only an unjustifiable dogmatism pronounces with certainty on the insoluble difficulty of the different records when biblical scholars differ.

In John's Gospel the apocalyptic element passes almost entirely out of sight. The term "kingdom" is supplemented by "eternal life." The coming of Christ is spiritual as manifested at Pentecost, in the Christian's personal experience of the saving power of Christ, his coming at the death of the Christian, and his final parousia for the judgment.

THE LAPSE OF TIME

Some eminent scholars claim that those who had looked for an earlier coming of the Messiah had misunderstood him, for he specifically enumerates certain experiences to be undergone and certain tasks to be accomplished before the Kingdom can come. In both Matthew and Mark the declaration is made that before the downfall of Jerusalem and the second advent the "good news" must be "preached to all the nations" and that "nation will rise against nation."

Time is allowed for false messiahs and prophets. "And when you shall hear of wars and rumors of war, be not troubled. They must come to pass, but not yet is the end." How can these declarations be harmonized with, "Ye shall not have gone through the cities of Israel till the Son of man be come"? Christ's parables of the leaven and mustard seed indicate some lapse of time.

Those who hold to a verbal dictation theory and

literal inerrancy resort to sophistry in an effort to make a forced harmony of the Scriptures. Intellectual honesty admits the uncertainty as to the exact words of Jesus. This does not result in any uncertainty as to the revelation of the essential saving truths of the Gospel. No biblical scholar has yet been able to reconcile all of the passages which have to do with the fall of Jerusalem and the coming of Christ. But regardless of differing opinions at this point, we may be confident of one thing, that a thousand years physical reign of Christ on earth is no part of the Christian doctrine.

According to the whole tenor of the teachings of Jesus, the second coming is immediately antecedent to the final judgment. No interval is allowed for any visible earthly reign of Jesus. An inductive study of the New Testament affords a complete refutation of Adventism.

It would appear to be a very doubtful performance to put one figurative passage in a highly figurative book against the clear and explicit statements of the Gospels. Adventists see a thousand years throughout the Scriptures, but it is only by a sleight-of-hand interpretation.

IN THE LAST DAYS

A further question relates to the spiritual condition of the world in the "last days." The siren voice of the reconciler can only deal in sophistry. Some scriptures indicate an increasing wickedness. Jesus is reported as raising the question of whether he would find faith on the earth. Paul in his second letter to Timothy discloses that evil men and imposters shall wax worse and worse, deceiving and being deceived.

On the other hand, Jesus promises that every plant which his heavenly Father has not planted shall be rooted up. Paul declares that Jesus must reign until he has put all his enemies under his feet. Since no consistent picture is drawn, dogmatism has no place.

But apart from all of the contrasted passages, the Christian Gospel is one of power and hope. Victory belongs to Christ, even though it is in the far future. When we reckon not by years and decades, but by the centuries, we see the steady progress of the good and catch the vision

> "Of the one far-off divine event
> To which the whole creation moves."

IV

CRUDE LITERALISM

CONTROVERSY HAS VERY DECIDED LIMITATIONS IN the accomplishment of good results. Men are largely dominated by prejudice and preconceived notions rather than by reason. As stated in the "Foreword," the purpose of this volume is a preventive rather than a cure. The Adventist falls into an obsession in which he imagines that any opposition to his opinion is an attack on the Christian faith.

TURNING THE BIBLE INTO A RIDDLE

We have good people who fall victims to so-called Bible teachers who have wasted a large portion of their lives counting the numbers and the horns in Daniel and Revelation. What can you do with people who turn the Bible into a riddle book and are sure they have solved the riddle? When some of our own members who are not informed in the true method of biblical interpretation listen to these Adventist advocates with their inane juggling of figures, they exclaim, "How perfectly marvelous! We never understood it before." What can be truer than figures? It is strange that all the world does not cry crystal.

The seven times of Leviticus 26:18 are interpreted to mean 2,520 years, on the ground that the words denote seven-year periods of 360 days each, and that the days are to be further translated into years. A similar absurdity is practiced in the "three and a half times" of Daniel, and the "forty-two months" of Revelation. Charts are constructed which are fearfully and wonderfully made. The "seven times" of Leviticus simply means that the punishment of Israel is to be seven times proportional to the transgression.

But William Miller adds 2,520 years to the 677 B.C., the date of the captivity of Manasseh, and comes out at A.D. 1843, the time of the final consummation. Pastor Russell adds the 2,520 years to 606 B.C., the date of Nebuchadnezzar's conquest of Israel and comes out at A.D. 1914. Yet each cocksure Adventist has the key that unlocks the future. They make anything mean anything they want it to mean.

Adventism deals in isolated proof texts and disconnected words and phrases. As is readily seen, it is a mixture of the literal and fanciful method of dealing with the Scriptures. The witty but true observation has been made that a text without the context is a pretext. By ignoring the context the Adventists prove anything to their own satisfaction. By that method of interpreting Scripture you can prove that you should hang yourself at once. "Judas went out and hanged himself." "Go thou and do likewise." "What thou doest, do quickly." A literalist who had read the saying of Jesus, "If thy right hand offend thee, cut it off, and cast it from thee," went into the woodshed, cut off his right hand, and threw it away. His family had him put in the insane asylum.

The Seventh-Day Adventist is a typical literalist. He keeps Saturday for his Sabbath according to the Old Testament. He believes in a kind of soul-sleeping, because Paul speaks of death as sleep.

A FAILURE OF DISCRIMINATION

A marked feature of literalism is that it has no sense of discrimination between the temporary and permanent elements of the Scriptures. Paul gives the injunction that women keep silent in the churches. Due to pagan surroundings and custom, this was necessary to protect the influence of the Church. The effort was made by literalists to make this rule permanent, but it had to be abandoned as hopeless. The further injunction was, "And if they will learn anything, let them ask their husbands at home." In many instances today, this would indicate that the wives who are at church should ask their husbands who stayed at home what the preacher meant in a certain part of the sermon.

THE BLIGHT OF LITERALISM

The verbal inspiration of the Scriptures, with the consequent notion of mechanical inerrancy, is thoroughly discredited in the mind of any intelligent student of the Bible who is willing to face the facts. This dead-level conception of the Bible is refuted by Jesus, who calls attention to the imperfection of the earlier revelation: "It has been said to you by them of old, but I say unto you. . . . ."

Consistently applied, this theory lowers our ethical ideals by elevating the old principles of revenge, slavery, polygamy, and militarism to the level of the Sermon on the Mount. Jesus revealed the perfect standard and declared the imperfection of certain Old Testament passages. The theory of a mechanical verbal inspiration places the Old Testament on the same level with the New. Instead of being truly orthodox, it is the denial of the authority of Jesus Christ.

A theory that holds to a dead-level revelation results in un-Christian ethics. Adventists construe the slaughter of women and infants on the part of

Joshua as following the direct command of God. They defend the imprecatory psalms, and the imprecatory prayers will find their complete fulfillment in the punishment inflicted by Christ on his enemies at his second coming. The true idea of a progressive revelation does not attribute to God the imperfect morality of portions of the Old Testament.

We are shut up to the alternative of accepting the imperfect stages of a progressive revelation or an imperfect God. The theory of the Adventists commits them to a belief in an imperfect God. If we are to believe in the God whom Jesus reveals we are to understand that the crude and cruel passages of the Old Testament do not express the mind of God. The Anglican Church excluded the imprecatory psalms as being "most un-Christlike in character and an insult to the divine majesty." John Wesley omitted them from the book of worship which he prepared for The Methodist Church in America as "highly improper for the mouths of a Christian congregation."

A MIXTURE OF THE LITERAL AND FANCIFUL

When the charge of a crude literalism is made against the Adventists, it is necessary to explain that they are not consistent literalists. They swing from the literal to the fanciful and back again as it

43

suits their purpose. If the literal does not suit their fancy, they go to the fanciful. And if the fanciful does not please their fancy, they resort to the literal. The transition from the literal to the fanciful is seen in the *Scofield Bible*. This Bible has footnotes by the editor, Dr. C. I. Scofield, and was first published in 1909. It is the standard authority of Adventism.

Some people regard the interpretation of Dr. Scofield as the Law and the Gospel. If you will read simply the scriptural portion of this Bible, you are on safe ground, for it is the Authorized Version. But Dr. Scofield's footnotes carry the impression of an exegetical magician. He can throw a rope in the air and climb it with agility hand over hand. How illuminating to the initiated is his comment on Gensis 41:45. "Asenath, the Gentile bride espoused by Joseph, is the type of the Church called out from the Gentiles." Is not this clear and convincing? Why should you question it? Did not Dr. Scofield say so? This is only one example taken at random from hundreds of notions equally absurd. We are not surprised that Dr. A. T. Pierson and Dr. J. M. Gray formerly of the Moody Bible Institute were his consulting editors. The *Scofield Bible* is one of the most subtle agencies for Adventist propaganda. The peril is that the

uninstructed reader will confuse the idiosyncrasies
of Scofield with the meaning of Scripture.

Adventism produces rationalism. It is a case
where extremes meet. It nourishes the rationalist
whom it seeks to destroy. The increasing intelligence of people is making a literalistic acceptance
of the Bible more and more impossible. If an intelligent faith is ignored by preachers and the people
are confronted with the alternative of a super-
stitious belief or the denial of the faith, the choice
will at last be made of rationalism.

To take the Bible, with its vital and spiritual
revelation, the moral message of the great prophets,
the Sermon on the Mount, the high spiritual alti-
tudes of the apostolic epistles, and pass them by
with little emphasis in order to juggle with figures
and numbers in apocalyptic passages is the acme of
folly.

A FEVERISH EXPECTATION

Adventism has resulted in wild fanaticism and
fanatical movements. The year A.D. 100 was set
for the end of the world, and also several dates in
the sixteenth century, and various dates were fixed
in the nineteenth century. William Miller lectured
through New England on the prophecies of the
Bible, and by making use of its symbolism convinced thousands that the world would come to

an end in A.D. 1843. Some prepared ascension robes that they might be ready for the coming of the Lord. He changed the date to 1844. Pastor Russell fixed the time of universal peace at A.D. 1914.

The advocates of Adventism learn nothing from the lessons of the past. It has been refuted by nineteen centuries of Christian history. Many saintly characters from the first through the succeeding centuries were confident that they were living in the last days, but the evident fact is they were mistaken. Nineteen centuries of mistakes certainly constitute no argument for the truth of a theory.

Adventists in the face of false predictions of the past have become somewhat more wary as to fixing an exact date in the future for the end of the world. The indications are that very many who hold that we are on the verge of the consummation of earthly affairs are not willing to base their own material future on their professed belief.

Dr. S. Parkes Cadman gives a suggestive instance in connection with a neighbor in Brooklyn who had fixed the date for the end of the world. This neighbor owned a valuable home. Dr. Cadman offered his neighbor a price which was beyond the value of the property, with the understanding that he would pay cash, and not take possession until after the date when the world was to come to an end. Of course the neighbor was not supposed to have any further use for his house. However, he emphatically refused the offer of Dr. Cadman.

Dr. Georgia Harkness relates the incident of an Adventist who refused to send his son to college, since the end was so near. It never occurred to the brother that since the world was soon to end, he would have no further use for his money.

In the northern part of Pennsylvania, years ago, there lived a man who confidently expected that Jesus would come again during his lifetime. So he made a will leaving his farm and home to Jesus Christ. His hope and expectation was that the Lord would build the New Jerusalem on his land.

Adventism has given rise to many fanatical movements. When I was abroad—this may be the only opportunity of making use of these delightful words—when I was abroad for the first time, I stopped in Jerusalem at the American Colony Hotel. Some years ago a group of Americans came prepared with ascension robes for the second coming of Jesus on the Mount of Olives. Following their disappointment, they turned their venture into a business enterprise and built the hotel.

THE ANTIDOTE FOR FANATICISM

The undiscerning reader is impressed by the abundance of scriptural quotations on the part of

Adventists and fail to reckon with a correct exegesis.

Literary form must be considered. The imagination and metaphors of poetry must not be literally construed. Figurative expressions are used in all languages and they flourish with great luxuriousness in the East. Much confusion and damage would have been avoided if interpreters of the Bible had given heed to Paul's words, "The letter killeth, but the spirit giveth life."

It is certainly not loyalty to the Scriptures to construct a whole system of doctrine on one passage in Revelation which puts its truth in the form of symbols. The literalist does violence to the Scriptures. In consistency the literalist should attempt to measure the magnitude of the woman in the seventeenth chapter of Revelation, who "sat upon seven mountains." Adventists "fashion a creed out of poetic imagery." They construct a system of doctrines out of symbols.

Historical scholarship in the study of biblical literature faces a series of questions: the authorship, date when it was written, to whom it was written, the purpose of writing, and the essential content of the writer's message. The historical method is far from sophistry, does not juggle with words, but seeks to discover the real meaning and purpose of the author. Historical scholarship does not regard the Bible as a storehouse of proof texts, but as a holy record of man who sought God and found him, and of God who sought man and found him —a holy record which brings us face to face with God and his way and his truth and his will.

V

THE CHANGE OF ATMOSPHERE

THE REACTIONISM OF ADVENTISM MAY BE OB-
served in two similar and yet different manifesta-
tions. First it runs counter to the large preponder-
ance of biblical scholarship. In the second place,
there is the refusal to think in terms of our present
scientific knowledge.

BIBLICAL SCHOLARSHIP

A half century and more ago, some illustrious
scholars were Adventists, but today the opposition
by scholars is practically unanimous. The historical study of each book in its historical setting has
sounded the death knell of premillennialism. A
score of years ago Dr. J. H. Snowden obtained official information from twenty-seven leading theological schools in eight denominations and found
that of 236 members of faculties, only eight were
premillennialists. In the past twenty years this
number has been further reduced. The trend is

28292

manifest in such works as Hastings' *Dictionary of the Bible*, Hastings' *Dictionary of the Apostolic Church*, *The Abingdon Commentary*, *A New Commentary on Holy Scripture* (edited by Dr. Charles Gore and two associates), *The Expositor's Greek Testament*, *The International Critical Commentary*, Moffatt's *New Bible Commentary*, and the constant stream of theological books by biblical scholars. The verdict of biblical scholarship has been largely against Adventism from the time of Origen until now.

Origen, the greatest scholar of the Greek Church, rejected premillennialism, declaring that those who accept it "understand the Scriptures in a sort of Jewish sense, deriving from them nothing worthy of the divine promises." Today the leading representatives of all of the large denominations do not accept the theory.

SCIENTIFIC KNOWLEDGE

Adventism not only runs counter to biblical scholarship, but refuses to think in terms of scientific knowledge. It retains a persistent prejudice against all new knowledge. We are afflicted both with the antireligionist in science who thinks that science is the panacea for all human ills and the antiscientist in religion who refuses to accept the verified findings of scientific knowledge. We are

51

now concerned with this latter type. Nature has a way of disposing of types of life that do not adapt themselves to changing conditions. We are informed that the dinosaur lived about ninety million years ago, was seventy feet long, with a skull as large as an elephant's but a brain inside as small as a man's thumb. This huge monster was not violently disposed of, but passed out when it failed to adapt itself to a changed situation. No one killed the monster. The climate changed and it died. This principle applies to opinions and beliefs as truly as to animals. Adventism is persisting even in a transformed intellectual and spiritual atmosphere, but its days are numbered. Adventism could thrive as a natural growth when the idea prevailed that the earth was about four thousand years old at the time of Christ, and that the earth was the center of the universe. We may question some of the large figures of science, but there are sufficient verified findings to result in changing our mental climate. The calculation is that the world began something like two billion years ago, which is several hundred thousand times the length of all recorded history and more than a million times the length of the Christian Era.

A very curious mental attitude is that so long as the world was regarded as of a few thousand years' duration, it seemed to be old. When the time was estimated at the beginning of the Christian Era as four thousand years, it seemed to be so old as to be on the verge of dissolution. When it reached the age of five thousand, the prevalent opinion was that such senility and decrepitude could not continue and that it was destined to collapse as the deacon's one-horse shay. It is a very old world today to those who close their minds against all new knowledge. How can such a Methuselah world be expected to survive much longer? But, strange to say, when scientists calculated its continuance in terms of multiplied millions of years, the earth renewed its youth. The change of atmosphere was such that with the conception of the vast stretch of time the world became young, and Tennyson expressed its youthful vigor: "This fine old world of ours is but a child yet in the gocart."

> "We are the Ancients of the earth,
> And in the morning of the times."

INDICATIONS OF A LONG CONTINUANCE

The ages of the earth's past seem to have been a preparation for the life and mind which now is, and for the mind which is still to come. It has been a slow and laborious process. Faith is bound to suppose that there is some deep plan and meaning in it all, and that the ultimate outcome will demonstrate divine wisdom and purpose.

The astronomers tell us that our sun and every other star that we can see are continuously sending out radiant energy at a rate to stagger the imagination, and in so doing are gradually using up their supply. Though it may require fifteen billion years for the sun to lose one-tenth of one per cent of its mass at its present rate of energy expenditure, the final result is none the less certain. The sun and every star that now shines must one day cease to shine. Every one of these bodies was endowed with the store of energy upon which it has been drawing and continues to draw.

We do not intend to say that we have any certainty that some catastrophe may not end the existence of the earth tomorrow, but we are saying that the intellectual and spiritual atmosphere in which we live has been changed. The modern conception of the position and comparative size of our own planet inevitably produces a change in our thinking which must be different from what it was with old Ptolemaic ideas. The centuries of refuted prophecies of the last days and of the Second Coming of Christ are a strong indication that many centuries more are to follow. The fact of a steady progress in the past is a promise of future progress as God continues to pour his life into humanity. Science can speak no authoritative word as to the nearness or remoteness of the end of the world. Science does affirm that there is no evident reason why the earth should not abide for millions of years.

Adventism breathes an alien atmosphere when time is expressed in terms of geological ages and astronomical cycles. The day of the final consummation of all earthly affairs is a matter of conjecture. I prefer the conjecture that our earth is fairly in its beginning rather than the conjecture of Adventists which past prophecies have proved false. The world is in its infancy rather than in old age and decrepitude.

The advocates of Adventism denounce all scientific scholarship as infidelity, unmindful of the fact that a scientific fact, when it is a fact is a revelation of the mind of God. Adventists are unable or unwilling to make the transition from the old and obsolete to the new conception. For some years yet earthly calamities will result in the same old order of prophecies of the immediate end of the present order of things.

But Adventism has no long lease on life. The more general dissemination of biblical and scientific knowledge will render the doctrine impossible. The atmosphere has changed, and Adventism cannot survive.

VI

THE NATURE OF PROPHECY

THE PROPHECIES OF SCRIPTURE AFFORD A PROB-
lem for interpretation. One group of scholars
strive to eliminate whatever savors of the supernatural, and attach no significance to the predictive element. Another group place their entire
emphasis on the element of prediction, and practically base their faith on the literal fulfillment of
the most minute and obscure prophesies. The
prophecies for them are oracles that map the future
events of the world.

The true solution appears to be that while prophecy has the element of prediction, yet in the main
the prophets bring a moral message to their own
contemporaries. This conception on the part of
biblical scholars arises from the historical method
of Bible study and is against a crude supernatural-
ism, but not against the supernatural.

The prophecy of the coming Messiah permeates
the Old Testament; yet it is not so much by specific

references to different events in his life, but by the forecast of the glorious age of deliverance, by the sense of incompleteness, by the aspiration of the soul of prophetic literature for the coming Redeemer.

CONTRASTED METHODS

The two distinct ways of interpreting the prophecies are the "modernizing" and the historical.

The historical method is the one employed by recognized biblical scholars and reckons with the purpose, meaning, and historical setting of the books of the Bible. The modernizing procedure of Adventism falls into the most ludicrous absurdities. The old idea of a prophet as a man to whom God had unrolled the scroll of the future goes by the board as soon as the historical approach is made. Some of the vagaries of the "modernizing" method are noted.

The National Recovery Act is clearly prophesied, according to this system, in the seventeenth verse of the thirteenth chapter of Revelation: "No man might buy or sell save he that had the mark . . . . of the beast." We are made to wonder what profit it could have been to his own generation for the Revelator to furnish it with information that the N.R.A. would be set up in the twentieth century.

An Adventist writer devotes a chapter to the

marvelous prophecy of the automobile in Nahum
2: 4. "The chariots shall rage in the streets, they
shall jostle one against another in the broad ways;
they shall seem like torches, they shall run like the
lightnings."

In the blessings of the twelve tribes in the thirty-
third chapter of Deuteronomy it is said of Asher,
"Let him dip his foot in oil." This is a prophecy
of prosperity for the tribe of Asher. A few months
ago, an Adventist writer in the *Sunday School
Times* elaborates on the wonderful fulfillment of
prophecy. In the twentieth century pipelines of
oil run underneath that particular portion of the
possession of Asher which is shaped as a foot. What
a marvelous evidence of a prophecy coming to pass
that now Asher dips his foot in oil! He must be
an unbeliever who would dare deny this forecast
of a far-off event!

In the view of Adventists, the principal function of prophecy is to write history in advance.
The history of the World War as well as the present
European and Asiatic conflicts are recorded by the
authors of Daniel and Revelation. In the World
War the capture of Jerusalem was clearly foretold
in the fifth verse of the thirty-first chapter of
Isaiah, "As birds flying, so will the Lord of hosts
defend Jerusalem." Who would be so bold as to

question that this was a prophecy of airplanes and aviators?

AS APPLIED TO THE SECOND ADVENT

In advocacy of a theory, the premillennialists select various passages from the Old Testament containing the word "come" and in violation of every true method of exegesis leap over the centuries and apply it to the second coming of Christ. All prophecies must be literally fulfilled, and since some of the supposed messianic prophecies were not fulfilled in the first coming of Jesus, they must be carried over to the second advent.

Many of the prophetic pictures were of the material prosperity and physical grandeur of the messianic kingdom. Judaic ideas of Christ's first coming are transferred to his second coming. Jesus did not come according to Jewish expectation; therefore his next coming will fulfill all of these expectations. Hundreds of passages in the Old Testament which by no stretch of the imagination can be referred to either coming are applied to the second coming. This abuse of reason and misuse of Scripture has no support in sane biblical interpretation, which has regard for the context and explicit meaning of Scripture. With the Adventists the Bible becomes a sort of crazy-quilt mixture of unrelated material.

BONDAGE TO SENSATIONALISM

The Adventists fall into a literalism which interprets the second coming in a spectacular manner which is not consistent with loyalty to the real meaning of the Scriptures.

We must allow the Scriptures to explain the Scriptures. "The kingdom of God cometh not with observation." If we are to be true to the Bible itself, we must reckon with its use of symbolic language. If we are willing to believe the Scriptures themselves, we must recognize that spectacular phenomena did not take place in literalistic fashion.

In the thirteenth chapter of Isaiah, the prophet is describing the downfall of Babylon. He says: "For the stars of heaven and the constellations thereof shall not give their light; the sun shall be darkened in its going forth, and the moon shall not cause its light to shine." This did not literally happen. Isaiah, in the reference given, pictured the extinction of the great lights of the state as the darkening of sun, moon, and stars. This had come to pass in the fall of Babylon while nothing happened in the sky. The darkening of the sun, moon, and stars in Matthew 24:29 is transferred from Isaiah 13:10 and Ezekiel 32:7, where it enters into the prediction of the downfall of Babylon and Egypt and Bozrah.

The pictorial language is taken from the Old Testament. Why should the same language be figurative in the earlier expressions and literal in the New Testament expressions? Jesus was speaking to the Jews, who were familiar with the vivid symbolism of the prophets.

A further illustration may be given. After the wonderful outpouring of the Holy Spirit on the day of Pentecost, Peter stood up and gave the true explanation: "This is that which hath been spoken through the prophet Joel." He quotes in Acts 2:16-21, from Joel 2:28-31, and explicitly says that the prophecy was fulfilled in the experience of Pentecost. But the sun was not turned to darkness nor the moon to blood, nor were there signs of blood and fire and vapor and smoke. This was the prophetic method of describing an epochal scriptural event.

Christ comes in every great crisis of the Kingdom. He comes in the destruction of Jerusalem, at his resurrection, on the day of Pentecost, to the individual in the presence of the Holy Spirit, where two or three are gathered together in his name, and with his people always, even unto the end of the world. But beyond all these advents, there is the final coming, the ushering in of the perfected Kingdom.

THE TRUE IDEA

One of the most irrational features of Adventism is its perversion of prophecy. The great prophets were social and moral leaders who spoke primarily to the people of their own day. The predictive element grew out of the inherent moral laws of the world and the retribution that inevitably followed the violation of these laws. This enabled the prophets to forecast the doom and downfall of the contemporary corrupt nations. They did not draw a chart of remote future events. But the prophets have a pertinent message for our modern world, since the moral laws of God are unchanging. The prophet predicted not the remote but the immediate future, growing out of present conditions. Amos pronounced doom on Israel while the nation was at the height of her political powers.

The message of the prophet is aimed at the specific evils in the life about him. He arises in days of national crisis and speaks his mind—or the mind of God—upon particular events. He denounces kings to their faces for specific acts, rebukes bluntly the mighty of the earth, and rebukes the people for their idolatries. His message is red-hot words out of a red-hot heart directed to a red-hot situation.

The prophets were not simply discovering these truths by the unaided strength of their own minds. They were thinking God's thoughts after him. Amos says, "The Lord God hath spoken, who can but tell it forth to others?" The moral insight of the prophet made the spiritual contribution of a growth in the conception of God, and brought about the transition from group to personal morality; and with the development of the individual personality, the way was prepared for social morality and the condemnation of the oppression of the poor. The Hebrew prophets were primarily advocates and champions of the poor and the exploited people of Israel, and were protesting against unjust and cruel economic conditions fostered by corrupt political leaders. They gave to the world the revelation of a righteous God, who demands of men personal and social righteousness. It is utterly false to suppose that they were endeavoring to pry into the happenings of our modern world.

Against the doctrine of Adventism, the primary purpose of prophecy is not prediction. This is a false etymology. Dr. Richard Moulton in the *Modern Readers' Bible for Schools* says, "The 'pro' in 'prophecy' is not the 'pro' that means beforehand, as in 'programme,' but the other 'pro' that means in place of, as in 'pronoun.' As a 'pronoun' is a word used in place of a noun, so a 'prophet' is one who speaks in place of God, a mouthpiece or interpreter of God. This is the regular use of 'prophet' in the Old Testament. It is the significance of the Greek word 'prophet,' and also of the Hebrew words which in the Greek Bible, or Septuagint, are replaced by the word 'prophet.' To quote only a single authority, Smith's *Bible Dictionary*: 'Etymologically it is certain that neither prescience nor prediction is implied by the term used in the Hebrew, Greek, or English language. To say this is not to say that Old Testament prophecies do not contain predictions. But the modern change in the use of this word has led to overemphasis upon the predictive element, which has obscured the other and more spiritual meaning of the term.' "

Another acknowledged authority may be quoted. Dr. George Adam Smith reinforces the declaration of Dr. Moulton. He writes, "In common use the name 'prophet' has degenerated to the meaning of one who foretells the future. . . . . In its native Greek, prophet meant 'one who speaks for or on behalf of' another. . . . . He is a speaker for God. . . . . Prediction of the future is only a part, and often a subordinate and accidental part, of an office whose full function is to declare the character and will of God."

The great prophets reach down to the present and to all coming time, not with a magical sort of foresight, but with a message from God that is eternally applicable to individuals and society.

VII

A FALSE CONCEPTION OF THE KINGDOM OF GOD

THE ADVENTISTS CLING TO A MATERIAL IDEA OF the messianic King and the Kingdom which is a repetition of the mistake of Jewish expectation. They claim that Jesus will occupy the throne of David and rule for a thousand years.

Adventism is Judaic in its dream of the restoration of the old Jewish nationalism. It is the old materialistic idea of the pomp of a world empire, with its capital at Jerusalem. When Jesus spoke of his Kingdom his hearers thought of an earthly kingdom of temporal power and material grandeur, and modern Adventists have fallen into the same mistake.

THE RESTORATION OF THE JUDAIC RITUAL

It is so grotesque as to be almost unbelievable that some prominent Adventists anticipate that with the second advent even the animal sacrifices will be restored. They are committed to this absurdity through their belief in the literal fulfillment of the letter of prophecy. Since the description, for example, in Ezekiel (chaps. 40 and 48) of the Jewish ritual and sacrifice was not consummated, it must come to pass in the millenial age. Dr. C. I. Scofield predicted the restoration of all the fundamental institutions of Israel. Strange to say, even so eminent a preacher as Dr. G. Campbell Morgan stated that while in the past the sacrifices and oblations pointed on to Christ, these restored in the millennium will be offered in memory of the work which Jesus accomplished on the cross. Such is the length to which good men will go in support of an impossible notion.

THE METHOD OF ESTABLISHING THE KINGDOM

Absolute reliance is placed in the physical force of militarism. The brutality of militarism loses none of its real hideousness by being attributed to the divine plan. The transformation of the compassionate Christ into a bloody conqueror is the most colossal crime in the entire history of theological thought. The blasphemy of infidelity in depicting the despotic cruelty of God fades into a meek gentleness compared with the picture that some premillennialists draw of Jesus. Adventists look for a Christ of fire and sword and blood, who shall march to his throne over the trampled bodies of his enemies.

This theory discredits the gospel of redemption, discounts the cross of Christ, and minimizes the Holy Spirit. It places its confidence in the power of a military Christ and loses sight of the fact that the strongest power in our world is spiritual. The Kingdom of God is a spiritual reality which cannot be created by outward physical force. The conversion of the individual and the world is a spiritual process and can be accomplished only by spiritual power. "Ye shall receive power when the Holy Spirit is come upon you." An Adventist writer says, "Christ now exhorts men to be holy; he will then demand holiness of men."

The true conception of the coming of the Son of Man is full of hope, and looks for the progress and ultimate triumph of the Kingdom of God on earth according to the prophetic statement: "Not by might nor by power, but by my spirit, saith the Lord." God is spirit, and the ultimate victory of right is to be won by spiritual power and not by physical brutality. Adventism is in reality defeatism. Adventism is a system of fatalism and makes such an overemphasis of the sovereignty of God as to leave no place for human co-operation in promoting the progress of the Kingdom of God. At the Conference at Edinburgh, an Edinburgh student in describing the theological viewpoint of an element in the Conference parodied the lines of the hymn by Dr. W. P. Merrill,

> "Rise up, O men of God!
> Have done with lesser things,"

to,

> "Sit down, O men of God!
> You cannot do a thing."

The travesty is still more grotesque that would write into our hymns the cruel treatment of his enemies by the Christ of the second advent. How would Christ as a military conqueror trampling his enemies under foot sound in song? Christ and the angels engaged in bloody warfare would produce a hymnology after the pattern:

> "Hark! the herald angels pass,
> Dropping bombs and poisonous gas."

We cannot conceive of this doctrine set to music and sung by a Christian congregation.

A HOPELESS GOSPEL

Adventists contend that they declare a gospel of hope, since God through physical force and by the exercise of an absolute sovereignty will set up the Kingdom. The readers are familiar with the oft-quoted declaration of Dr. R. A. Torrey: "As awful

69

as conditions are across the waters, and as awful as they may become in our country, the darker the night gets the lighter my heart gets." A belief, however, that is based on a combination of despair for the present and an illusory hope for the future can hardly be termed optimistic. The Christian hope must be based on the faith that God through spiritual force and spiritual processes will bring increasing victory to the good.

A SUPERFICIAL EVANGELISM

The Adventists express no hope for the conversion of the world through the preaching of the gospel. They draw a distinction between "converting the world" and "evangelizing the world." To evangelize is simply to proclaim the gospel for the purpose of making up the number of the elect preparatory to the coming of Christ. There is no hope of constructing a Christian civilization, but only of rescuing the elect. We have no evidence as to why this process was necessary for selecting the elect. The favorite passage is, "The gospel shall be preached in the whole world for a testimony unto all nations."

The coming of Christ is to be hastened by the mere proclamation of the gospel to the nations. This method has without question produced a missionary activity, but there is the absence of the highest spiritual motive. Adventism holds that despite the preaching of the gospel the world is to grow continually worse, and that the conversion of the world is conditioned on the second advent, when supernatural might shall smite down all opposition; the world cannot be saved through spiritual agencies. The theory of Adventism faces an insurmountable difficulty in the Great Commission of Jesus to his disciples: "All authority hath been given unto me in heaven, and on earth. Go ye therefore, and make disciples of all the nations, baptizing them in the name of the Father, and of the Son, and of the Holy Spirit: teaching them to observe all things whatsoever I have commanded you; and lo, I am with you always, even unto the end of the world." To make disciples certainly involves more than a hurried proclamation of the gospel for the purpose of gathering up the elect. To make disciples of all nations is evidently more than a superficial evangelistic proclamation of the gospel.

The Adventists are so hard beset by this passage that they substitute "out of" for "of" so as to read "make disciples out of all nations." This is to say that the elect are to be selected out of all nations. The Adventist perversion of the text is contrary to the plain construction of the Greek. Just so long as this doctrine is preached it will act as a brake on the wheels of progress and prove to be a serious obstacle in the way of the full realization of the Kingdom of God on earth. It is a pessimism darker than death and deeper than the grave.

VIII

THE TRUE CONCEPTION OF THE KINGDOM OF GOD

THE ADMISSION IS TO BE FREELY MADE THAT some of the declarations of Jesus concerning the Kingdom are in the framework of apocalyptic symbols. These, however, do not veil the vital elements of the teaching of Jesus.

We have seen in the preceding chapter that Jesus gave no endorsement of the Jewish expectation of a material messianic reign which would be achieved through physical might. The spiritual character of the Kingdom is predominant.

EMPHASIS ON THE KINGDOM

The Kingdom of God is the great term which Jesus employs more than any other. He uses it eight times in the Sermon on the Mount and one hundred and twelve times in the four gospels. The larger number of parables are parables of the Kingdom. He commissioned the twelve and the

seventy disciples to preach the gospel of the Kingdom. This was the first and last note of his preaching and teaching. "Repent, for the Kingdom of
Heaven is at hand," was the exhortation that
marked the beginning of his ministry. In the
forty days following the resurrection he spoke to
his disciples concerning the Kingdom.

THE CHURCH AND THE KINGDOM

Early in Christian history the Church came to
receive the major emphasis. The exaltation of the
Church above the Kingdom is out of accord with
the mind of Jesus. The Church is the agency for
the promotion of the Kingdom. The Kingdom is
the end to which the Church is the means. The
Kingdom is larger and more inclusive than any
church or than all the churches. The Kingdom
is more exclusive than the Church, since the Church
may contain members who are actual enemies of
the Kingdom.

VARYING IDEAS

Some three ideas of the Messiah, the King of the
Kingdom, belong to prophetic and apocalyptic
literature. First, he was to be the political and
military successor of David to a material throne.
Second, he was to usher in the Kingdom as the
Son of Man on the clouds of heaven. Third, he

was to win his dominion as the Suffering Servant through the vicarious sacrifice of the cross. These three conceptions were current in the time of Jesus.

The first idea was held by the Pharisees and Zealots and is held by modern Adventists. Adventism combines the first with the apocalyptic feature of the second. Jesus rejected the first in the wilderness temptation. He introduces the apocalyptic element of the second, but places major emphasis on the third ideal of his vicarious death on the cross.

In John's Gospel the apocalyptic element almost entirely disappears. The Kingdom is not an object of physical vision, but is the spiritual life of man. "Except a man be born from above, he cannot see the Kingdom of God." Jesus chose the spiritual rather than the material ideal of the Kingdom. The attitude of the disciples was expressed in their disappointment, "We had hoped that it was he which should redeem Israel."

The crucifixion of Christ produced the collapse of faith in Christ. His claim to be the Son of God was refuted by the very fact that God did not come to his rescue and that he was not able to save himself. If his career had ended on the cross, then the cross could never have become the symbol of his redeeming power. The cross would have been the terminus of a blind alley. The resurrection transformed the doubt and despair of the disciples into a buoyant hope. "He was crucified in weakness, but raised in power." "He was declared to be the Son of God with power by his resurrection from the dead." The promise of the coming of the Spirit was realized in the experience of the disciples. They went forth after Pentecost in the power of the Spirit to establish on earth the Kingdom of God.

The gospels and epistles make central the spiritual nature of the Kingdom. The Kingdom of God will come through the spiritual transformation of the individual and human society. In the place of diagrams and ingenious literal fulfillments of prophecy, we see a universe under the reign of a God of law and of love. The incomparable marvel of Christ is in his reliance on the omnipotence of love.

The Kingdom of God is the rule of God over the life that men live together. It is that divine order in which men live as sons of God and brothers of each other, the world-wide sway of justice and love and good will.

Jesus taught his disciples to pray "Thy kingdom come. Thy will be done, as in heaven, so on earth." The progress of the Kingdom is conditional on the measure of man's obedience to God's will.

THE BLENDING OF CONTRASTED IDEAS

The Kingdom of God is too large a conception to define. Description must take the place of definition.

The Kingdom is both present and future. The Adventists place the Kingdom solely in the future against the clear declaration of Jesus in which he refers to it as present. He said to the Pharisees, "The publicans and harlots go into the Kingdom before you." "Ye shut the Kingdom of heaven against men; for ye enter not in yourselves, neither suffer ye them that are entering in to enter." Again he said to the Pharisees, "If I by the Spirit of God cast out devils, then is the Kingdom of God come unto you." Jesus was asked by the Pharisees when the Kingdom of God should come. He replied, "The Kingdom of God cometh not with observation; neither shall they say, lo here, or lo there, for the Kingdom of God is in the midst of you."

In construing the Kingdom as a present reality, Jesus made a departure from the prevailing notions of his age. On the other hand, as reported in the gospels, he looked forward to the future for the coming of the Kingdom. "There be some of those standing here who will not taste death till they see the coming of God's Kingdom wtih power."

It may be frankly admitted that, in spite of the siren voice of the reconciler, the varying conceptions cannot be harmonized. We are left to choose that ideal of the Kingdom to which Jesus gave the most emphasis, and which history has made the most reasonable conception.

Another contrast is that the Kingdom is gradual in its growth and yet appears suddenly. There is the suddenness and immediacy of the Kingdom supernaturally inaugurated, "the Son of man coming on the clouds of heavens with power and great glory." We have also the gradual growth of the Kingdom. This growing conception is seen in the parables of the mustard seed and the leaven. The mustard seed represents the extension of the Kingdom and the leaven the intensive development of the spiritual life in humanity. The Kingdom is also compared to the growth of grain. "The earth bringeth forth fruit of herself; first the blade, then the ear, then the full corn in the ear."

We have the contrast of divine and human agencies. The supernatural action of God is required to bring in the Kingdom. Only the power of God can bring in the Kingdom of God. Yet the necessity for human effort remains, and human co-operation with God receives its sufficient motive power from the realization that the strength of God is back of weak human endeavors.

A further contrast is that the Kingdom is both individual and social. Jesus called upon men to "seek first the Kingdom of God." He said, "Blessed are the poor in spirit, for theirs is the kingdom of heaven." Paul described the Kingdom as "righteousness and peace and joy in the Holy Spirit." Jesus declares the supreme value of the Kingdom in the parables of the hidden treasure and the goodly pearl. These indicate an individual possession.

On the other hand, personality is developed only through social relationships. The family idea of the Kingdom, with God as Father and men as brothers, is emphasized. The family ideal is the co-operative rather than the competitive principle. It is here that our economic and social order is put to the test. The stronger members of the family are not supposed to snatch from the weaker members their due portion of material possessions. Jesus in the beginning of his ministry makes a declaration of his social program:

"The Spirit of the Lord is upon me,
Because he anointed me to preach good tidings to the poor;
He hath sent me to proclaim release to the captives;
And recovering of sight to the blind;
To set at liberty them that are bruised;
To proclaim the acceptable year of the Lord."

A PARADOX

The Kingdom of God is eternal and yet earthly. It is primarily spiritual and yet material. We are to be otherworldly to the extent of getting a glimpse of far-off horizons. We are to possess this-worldliness to the extent of applying the principles of the Kingdom to our earthly situation. Jesus said to Pilate, "My kingdom is not of this world." The simple meaning is that the Kingdom does not have a worldly origin. But while its origin it not here, yet the Kingdom is to be established in this world. As paradoxical as it may seem, the spiritual and the material are not in opposition to each other.

A spurious spirituality separates the spiritual from the material. The true spiritual riches are entrusted only to those who make a right use of the material things. By a sort of divine alchemy we are to transmute the baser metals of the material into the gold of the spiritual. The life in the bulb transforms the unclean soil into the beauty of the flower that surpasses the glory of Solomon's wardrobe. The energy of the black grimy coal is transformed into the radiance of the incandescent light. So the spiritual life of the Kingdom is to transform the stubborn material elements into spiritual beauty and glory. It is then that the poverty, squalor, and the misery of the earth will vanish.

INTERIM ETHICS

Whatever may have been the expectation of the

Early Church of the immediacy of the Kingdom, the fact is manifest that the principles of the Kingdom are of permanent validity and application. We can conceive of no increasing complexity of social and economic organization in which the command, "Love thy neighbor as thyself," would not be the best workable ideal for human society. However intricate and interwoven our organized life may become, the Golden Rule, the Sermon on the Mount, and human brotherhood are the only principles that will prevent our modern civilization from toppling over the precipice into destruction.

UNIVERSALITY

Jesus declared the universal range of the Kingdom of God. He renounced the nationalistic narrowness of the Jews. He asserted that many would come from the east and the west and find a place in the Kingdom. The gospel was to be preached unto all nations. The Kingdom of God is a supranational, supra-racial, and supra-class fellowship.

Paul declared that the middle wall of partition was broken down and the distinction removed between Jew and Gentile. The Kingdom knows no racial nor territorial limits. This concept of universality pervades the gospel. Its universality is made possible by its spirituality. All who repent, all who believe, all who exercise the childlike spirit,

81

and all who renounce the love of the world may enter the Kingdom. Spiritual agencies only can build a spiritual Kingdom.

The ideal is a universal Kingdom established through spiritual agencies. If we looked only on the dark phases of the present, we would fall into despair; but as we look across the long range of history from the Stone Age until now we see the clear steps of progress toward the ideals of Jesus Christ.

Toward this realization we are not to indulge in an easy-going optimism, with a creulous confidence in an automatic sort of progress; but with hearts strengthened by the hope of Christ we are to dedicate to him the unreserved devotion and sacrificial loyalty of our lives. There is the abiding hopefulness of the gospel. This hope is to persist against all discouragement and to rejoice in the better day that is coming to the world.

In the darkest hour that ever cast its shadow on our sinful earth Jesus said, "This gospel of the kingdom shall be preached in all the world." To lose the spirit of hope is to lose the spirit of Christ.

He is the Chief of all saintly spirits who

> "Rowing hard against the stream,
> See distant gates of Eden gleam,
> And do not dream it is a dream."

IX

THE KEY THAT UNLOCKS THE MYSTERY

AN UNDERSTANDING OF THE APOCALYPTIC LIT-erature which is not included in the biblical canon leads to an understanding of this form of literature. The general reader needs to know only the nature and purpose of the literature.

The advocates of Adventism have a total mis-understanding of apocalyptic literature. A study of this literature in its historical setting would re-lieve any sincere person of this heresy. The Jewish apocalypses are a group of writings that appear in the three centuries between 200 B.C. and A.D. 100. They were written for the encouragement of the people in bad times, when the strong forces of wick-edness were dominant and oppressive. These books did not find their way into the canon. The two distinctive apocalyptic books of the Bible are Daniel and Revelation. These served a good purpose for encouragement in evil days. The tragedy is now that Adventists give more emphasis to these two books than to all the rest of the Scriptures. Their interpretation is, like man, fearfully and wonderfully made. The books are treated with a complete neglect of the historical background.

Some scholars claim that when Israel came in contact with alien religions, especially that of Persia, which was based on an elaborate doctrine of the spiritual world, the Persian and Old Testament ideas were thrown together, and out of this intermingling there emerged the new type of thought which comes before us in the apocalyptic writings. The indications, however, are that this literature was largely of Jewish origin.

A knowledge of apocalyptic literature is essential for the study of the New Testament as also of the Old Testament, and the doctrines of the primitive Church cannot be understood without reference to the conceptions revealed in this literature.

FOR DARK DAYS

In a time when the night was darkest men encouraged their followers with the promise of a coming day. The significance of the word "apocalypse" is "an unveiling," a revealing of what is soon to come to pass. The day was speedily coming when Israel, oppressed and cruelly treated, would receive supernatural deliverance. These writings have been called tracts for bad times. With elaborate visions and symbols, the final overthrow of evil was pictured.

For the most part, the apocalyptic books from 200 B.C. to A.D. 100 did not find a place in the canon. Some of these books are the Psalms of Solomon, First and Second Maccabees, Enoch, the Assumption of Moses, Testaments of the Twelve Patriarchs, Wisdom, Esdras, and Baruch. The writers frequently use the assumed names of noted Hebrew characters. The safety of the writer is conditioned on concealing his own name and in veiling his references to the oppressing tyrants by employing symbols. It was safer to use the name of some notable hero of the past as the author. If perchance the book should fall into the hands of the oppressor, with all of his persecuting zeal, he would be unable to inflict vengeance on the dead.

The writers hurled their flaming indignation against the oppressors and the oppressive nations under the cover of symbols of beasts, which were understood by their faithful followers. By way of contrast, the prophets came face to face with wicked rulers in their stinging rebukes, as, for example, Elijah and Ahab. Neither prophets nor apocalyptists forecast the far future. A predictive element belongs in common to both types of writers, but the future events were near at hand and sprang out of the present.

A further feature of apocalyptic literature was its fatalism. The idea of the sovereignty of God reduced human co-operation to a minimum. The prophets gave more recognition to the human factor. The prophets placed more emphasis on the progress and future of the nation. The apocalyptist caught a vision of the eternal world beyond time.

The Book of the Secrets of Enoch develops the millennium theory which was to become so popular in after years. The world was created in six days, each day a thousand years, the seventh day being the duration of the temporal Kingdom, now viewed as the millennium. The day of judgment follows, the righteous going to their reward in Paradise, while the wicked are cast into hell. Baruch and Esdras, which are in the Old Testament Apocrypha, picture the impending end and God's punishment of the wicked. An apocalyptic element was in the teaching of Jesus, who announced the ultimate defeat of evil and the victory of the good in symbolic language.

It is a strange sort of reversal that the apocalyptic literature which served to preserve the religion of faith has become, in the hands of the modern literalists, a real though unintentional enemy of the faith. That which served the indispensable purpose of producing hope in its own day has become in our day a doctrine of despair. The dark days from the tyranny of Anitochus Epiphanes to the persecution by Rome were marked by these writings which held out the hope of deliverance. While the literal predictions were not fulfilled, yet it is highly probable that religious faith would not have survived but for the encouragement which these writings afforded. They encouraged faith in God and held out hope for the triumph of the good at a time when it was not possible to use a more spiritual medium. The apocalyptists looked forward to an immediate supernatural intervention and deliverance by miraculous physical might. The abiding spiritual value is the invincible faith in the ultimate triumph of right.

The true historical viewpoint reckons with the national crisis which caused the book to be written. With the picture of the early and certain overthrow of the oppressive evil forces the courage of the faithful was immensely fortified. Adventists miss the purpose of this type of literature and bend the words to fit their theory of a projection of the prophecy into the modern world. A knowledge of the historical setting of apocalyptic literature and its purpose is the key which unlocks the mysteries of the books of Daniel and Revelation.

X

THE PROPHET DANIEL

THE EARLIEST APOCALYPTIC LITERATURE IN ANY complete form was the Book of Daniel. Contrary to the traditional view, modern scholars agree that the Book of Daniel was written about 165 B.C., near the close of the reign of Antiochus Epiphanes, 175-164 B.C.

These scholars point out in favor of the late date several items of evidence. Daniel is in the third division of the canon, "The Writings." If a prophet of the sixth century had written the book it would have been placed in the second division, "The Prophets." Furthermore, the scholars inform us that the Hebrew of Daniel is of a late type. More Persian words are employed than a Hebrew writer would have used at the Babylonian court in the sixth century. The language of the book, both the Hebrew and Aramic, is much later than the Exile.

The use of Greek and Persian words indicates

a late date. The doctrinal ideas more closely resemble the Jewish writings of the second and first centuries B.C. than the earlier Old Testament books. Those who accept clear evidence such as this against the traditional date of Daniel are classed as religious infidels by Adventists. It is useless, however, to advance any evidence to people who naturally prefer fantasies to facts.

THE PURPOSE OF THE BOOK

In common with literature of this type, the purpose of the author was to encourage the devout Jews to adhere to their faith against the cruel aggressor and against the corrupting Greek influence. Antiochus placed a ban on Jewish religious observances—the Sabbath, temple sacrifices, circumcision, and the distinction of foods. He also had constructed on the site of the sacred altar of sacrifice an altar to Zeus and compelled the Jews to offer the sacrifice of swine. An image of the Greek god was set up in the court, which Daniel termed "the abomination that maketh desolate."

The author of the Book of Daniel reinforces the patriotic Maccabean movement to preserve the religious faith of the Hebrews. This background of historical setting is necessary to a right understanding of the book.

The book naturally falls into two parts. The

first six chapters relate the stories of Daniel and his three companions in the Babylonian exile. The second section, chapters 7-12, has been the fountain source of the vagaries of Adventism.

THE BEASTS

Our discussion will have to be limited to the particular features which have been misinterpreted.

The seventh chapter contains the vision of the four beasts: the first like a lion, another like a bear, another like a leopard, and the fourth beast with great iron teeth and ten horns and another little horn.

The critical scholars are in almost entire agreement to the effect that the four beasts represent successively the Babylonian, Median, Persian, and Greek kingdoms. The little horn in verse 8 stands for Antiochus Epiphanes of the Syrian portion of the divided Greek kingdom of Alexander. Antiochus was the arch enemy of God and his people and was termed by the Jews a madman or madcap.

In chapter eight Daniel records his vision of the ram and the goat. The ram represents the Medo-Persian power. The goat that appeared from the west and overthrew the ram, breaking his horns, is the description of Alexander's victorious career, coming out of Greece and conquering the Persian Empire.

The goat had one horn, which became four horns when Alexander's empire was divided among four of his generals. From the four horns sprang a little horn mentioned again in verse 9. The little horn as in the preceding chapter is Antiochus, who thought himself able to pluck the stars from their place, and defied God himself and caused the suspension of the temple services for more than three years.

The prediction of the downfall of Antiochus is in verse 25. "He shall be broken without hand." This prediction came to pass in 164 B.C. when Antiochus died on an expedition in Persia. The author had Daniel to put in the form of a prediction the doom that had fallen upon the first three beasts, and he encouraged the readers with a prophecy of the certain downfall of the tyrant Antiochus.

The purpose of the book has been grossly perverted by the arbitrary procedure of Adventism. As already stated, the beasts represent the earthly kingdoms, three of which had fallen, and the little horn of the fourth beast was in the time of the author warring against the saints. The exhortation is to remain steadfast, for the doom of the tyrant is near at hand.

The modernizing method that projects the vision of Daniel into the far future has no basis either in reason or Scripture. The Seventh-Day Adventists claim that the Church of Rome is the little horn of Daniel. How grotesque is the idea that the author of Daniel should encourage his readers courageously to resist the Roman Catholic Church. The designation of Hitler, Mussolini, or the Roman papacy as the beast and the prediction of their downfall could have been of no earthly or unearthly encouragement to the Jews who were suffering persecution.

JUGGLING WITH NUMBERS

Another much abused prediction has to do with the length of time before the cleansing of the sanctuary after its defilement. The predictions are not in entire agreement. In Daniel 7:25 the downfall of Antiochus and the cleansing will not take place "until a time and times and the dividing of time," or in three and a half years. In 8:14 the time is stated: "Unto two thousand and three hundred days; then shall the sanctuary be cleansed."

The number indicates evenings and mornings, or 1,150 days, a little less than three and a half years. In 12:11 the period of time is 1,290 days, or roughly three and a half years. This period of three and a half years is doubtless intended in all the different passages.

The Adventists take the 2,300 days and make the

days mean years. Why not? They are free to make anything mean anything.

According to Millerite chronology, when 2,300 years is added to the date of the decree of Artaxerxes for rebuilding Jerusalem, 457 B.C., the terminus of the period is A.D. 1843. When this time was reached the date was advanced to 1844, with the confession that an error was made in calculation. As the prediction for 1844 was not fulfilled, the explanation was that it was the heavenly and not the earthly sanctuary that was to be cleansed. Since this procedure places the predicted event out of sight and we cannot subpoena the angels, the Adventists remain undisturbed in their theory.

In Daniel 9:2 the desolation of Jerusalem is said to last for seventy years, according to the prediction of Jeremiah 23:10. Daniel implores God to look favorably upon the ruined sanctuary. The angel Gabriel explains to Daniel that it would not be seventy years, but seventy weeks of years, or 490 years. Jeremiah prophesied from about 625 to 595 B.C. The 490 years extend from the fall of Jerusalem, 586 B.C., bringing the end of the period to 96 B.C. The exact ending of the 490 years is not certain, since there was no exact chronology after the modern manner. The end of the period actually culminated in 164 B.C., the date of the death of Antiochus. Despite the impossibility of exactness as to dates, Daniel is dealing with his present and immediate future and is forecasting the cessation of the reign of terror of Antiochus.

MARVELOUS MATHEMATICS

Adventist interpretation as set forth in *Beacon Lights of Prophecy* projects the predictions of Daniel into the modern age. The little horn in chapter 7 is evidently Antiochus, and in 1,260 days he is to be overthrown. According to the marvelous mathematics of Adventism, the 1,260 days, which are made to mean years, when added to A.D. 538, the beginning of papal supremacy, bring us to 1798, when France put an end to the power of the Pope. What a wonderful prophecy it is! So it was not of Antiochus, but of the papacy that Daniel said, "He shall speak great words against the Most High."

Again as to the seventy weeks or 490 years, simply take sixty-nine of the weeks and add to 457 B.C., the date of the decree of Artaxerxes to Ezra, and it brings you to the time of Christ. The last week of the seventy includes the time in which we are now living, and culminates with the return of Christ in visible power and glory.

It is not possible to pursue the wild imaginings of the prognosticators. Any thoughtful reader will see the absurdity of Adventist calculations. Their whole procedure is utterly against any reasonable explanation of the Scriptures.

Scofield in his *Reference Bible* says that Daniel's vision sweeps the whole course of Gentile world-rule to its end in catastrophe and to the setting up of the messianic kingdom.

THE DAY OF TRIUMPH

It is not necessary to elaborate on the final vision of Daniel in chapters 10-13. In common with the preceding portion, the dark cruel figure of Antiochus is central, with the forecast of his downfall. The prediction was veiled and yet understood by the readers of the book. It afforded inspiration for patient endurance in the fiery furnace of persecution.

"One like the son of man came with the clouds of heaven. . . . . And there was given him dominion, and glory, and a kingdom, that all people, nations, and languages should serve him: his dominion is an everlasting dominion, which shall not pass away, and his kingdom that which shall not be destroyed." The figure of the son of man represents the saints of God, the purified human race, as is made clear in 7:22. "And judgment was given to the saints of the Most High; and the time came that the saints possessed the kingdom."

SPIRITUAL VALUES

Even with a prevalent misunderstanding of the Book of Daniel, some spiritual values appear on the surface. An unswerving loyalty to the truth is manifest. "Daniel purposed in his heart that he would not defile himself with the portion of the king's meat, nor with the wine which he drank." One of the sublimest utterances in all literature is the reply of Shadrach, Meshach, and Abednego to the angry King Nebuchadnezzar as they faced the burning fiery furnace. They said, in effect: "We need not waste any words in discussing this matter with you. If the God we worship is able or willing to deliver us from the fire, he will do so. But even if not we are resolved neither to serve the gods of Babylon nor prostrate ourselves before the king's image." Wrapped up in the words "but if not" is the noblest defiance ever uttered by a true faith against the command of a pagan political power.

When rightly interpreted the Book of Daniel has a pertinent message for our day, but not in the way of Adventism which would practically nullify its value. A tragic perversion of a great book is to turn it into a chart of a far-off future. The futuristic interpretation of Adventism has blinded the eyes of many Bible readers to its indispensable values.

The Book of Daniel served to preserve the faith of devout Jews in a time of desperate emergency. Strong emphasis is placed on the providential ruling of God over all the nations. The irresistible power of God is portrayed in 2:45: "The stone was cut out of the mountain without hands." The material might of nations with their feet of clay is at last powerless before this stone, the symbol of the Kingdom of God. The faith is nourished that, despite present indications, good is stronger than evil, God is stronger than all the forces of darkness, and ultimate victory is on the side of right.

> "Fierce though the fiends may fight,
> And long though the angels hide,
> We know that truth and right
> Have the universe on their side."

XI

THE BOOK OF REVELATION

THIS BOOK, WHEN RIGHTLY INTERPRETED, VINDI-
cates its value. No book of the Bible has been
more abused by the fantasies of fanatics. Many
questions must of necessity be passed over. The
authorship is uncertain. The author simply terms
himself "John," "John your brother." The dis-
ciple John always avoided the use of his own name.
I will have to limit myself to certain passages which
have been perverted by a fanciful interpretation.
The purpose is so to present the true viewpoint
that the bizarre notions of Adventism may be seen
to be without any reasonable support.

Revelation is the only book in the New Testament that is explicitly apocalyptic.

THE OUTLINE AND CONTENTS

In order that the reader may have a general
idea of the entire book, an outline is given:

I. The introduction and message to the seven
churches, chapters 1-3.

II. The assurance of victory in the vision of God on his throne, and of the Lion of the tribe of Judah, who is also the Lamb, chapters 4-5.

III. The three series of woes picturing the long, drawn-out conflict between the hosts of light and the forces of darkness: the fall of Rome and the overthrow of the beast and the false prophets, chapters 6-19.

IV. The victory of the Messiah, the defeat of the dragon, and the judgment of the dead, chapter 20. The vision of the Heavenly City and the conclusion, chapters 21-22.

THE PURPOSE AND HISTORICAL SETTING

The Book of Revelation is the final apocalyptic writing in the New Testament, dating from about A.D. 96 during the persecution of Domitian. The author writes with a widely different style and from a group of ideas far removed from those of the Fourth Gospel. He draws upon Jewish apocalyptic sources which are often out of harmony with the teaching of Jesus. The book pictures the severe persecutions of Christians by the Roman authorities, based on the demand of emperor worship. In the reign of Domitian, emperor worship was made a test of obedience to the state.

The purpose of the book was to strengthen the courage and faith of the Christian by visualizing the downfall of the Roman Empire and the final victory of the Kingdom of God and the victorious reign of Christ. The author writes from a situation that is apparently hopeless, when against the Church is arrayed the material might of Rome. The policy of Rome had been one of tolerance toward all religions; but when the Emperor Domitian issued an edict that divine honors should be paid to him, the Church refused, and persecution was the result. Instead of compromising on the idea that a ceremony expressing a worship of the emperor was only a patriotic declaration, the Christians refused to participate in what appeared to them to be a new form of idolatry.

Revelation served to inspire within the readers a courageous resistance even unto death against making God subordinate to the state. The Church is weak in itself, but the power of a God of omnipotence is the guarantee of victory. The message of the Apocalypse is a message for our modern world, but not a prediction of the modern age.

In the interpretation of Revelation, while not enumerating the different methods of interpretation, there are two distinct ways of approach. The first is the modernizing or futuristic method, and the second is the historical or literary.

THE FANTASTIC APPROACH

The first, the procedure of Adventism, works out a highly wrought chart and time calendar. We have the forecast of modern events and personalities: Napoleon, the Pope of Rome, Mussolini or Hitler. The future history of the Church is "a history of the Church in riddles." One prominent exponent of Adventism worked out the date of the second coming for April 11, 1901, at three o'clock in the afternoon, Jerusalem time. These predictions wriggle from one future date to another. Each forecaster has a key to the future, but it does not seem to fit the lock.

One is made to wonder how the Adventists persuaded themselves that a prediction of the rise and downfall of some modern pope or dictator could have been of any possible comfort and strength to the hard-pressed early Christians. The absurd injunction would be, "Hold out faithful to the end, for the Pope (or Mussolini or Hitler) will be shorn of his power." Calculators have wasted the labors of a lifetime in fantastic forecasts of the future. The Revelator explicitly declares in the opening verse that he is showing "things which must shortly come to pass."

The vain effort is made to read some modern significance into the various symbols. All reason is discarded and imagination runs riot. The person who naturally prefers an irrational sort of explanation can only be left to his choice.

For example, in chapter nine, the locusts were "like unto horses," with the "faces of men" and the "hair of women" and the "teeth of lions," with "breastplates of iron"; and "the sound of their wings was as the sound of chariots of many horses running to battle." "They had tails like unto scorpions, and there were stings in their tails"; and "they had a king over them, which is the angel of the bottomless pit," whose name is Abaddon or Apollyon. It is a vain effort to attach any significance to the details of this bizarre monster. The weird symbols were the trimmings drawn from apocalyptic literature and were never intended to obscure the main current of the author's thought.

But how clear it all becomes to the author of *Beacon Lights of Prophecy*. The locusts are a prophecy of the Saracen Conquest and Mohammedan force of the seventh century, A.D. Scofield in his *Reference Bible* and marvelous map of the future has the author in the letters to the seven churches coming down to the period of the Reformation in the message to Sardis. According to Scofield, the author is not addressing the contemporary churches, but churches in the distant future.

It is rather curious to apply the term modernizing to the Adventists. The explanation is that they project ancient events into the modern age. In every other respect they are ancient.

THE HISTORICAL METHOD

The second method of interpretation clearly shows that the Book of Revelation had nothing to do with a far distant future. Evidently the prediction in the book relates to the immediate and not the remote future, as the writer affirms in 1:1 and 22:6. The value lies not in disclosure of history in the nineteen following centuries nor of forecasts of still future events, but rather in its fitness to brace the Christian faith to meet one of the great crises of its history. When the writer speaks of "things shortly to come to pass" he means shortly. He is not concerned with the far-off centuries but with the urgent need of his own generation. The aim of the author is not a chronological program of world history, but to afford courage and hope to his own contemporaries.

The "modernizing" form of interpretation is being more and more discarded. The historical approach affords the only key for the right understanding of this book as well as for the Bible as a whole. From the viewpoint of the historical method, Revelation ceases to be a book of mystery and of enigmas. The author would have had no legitimate reason for writing a book which could not be understood by his contemporary readers. What the author is saying is that the power of God is supreme and that, in the present conflict between light and darkness, light will prevail. The oppressive Roman Empire would soon be overthrown, and the Church would emerge victorious. The central message of the book is plain.

Many Christians have been repelled from Revelation on account of the blending of the allegorical and literal interpretations of Adventism, so that the book has been abused on the one hand and neglected on the other. But we of today are in need of its message. While not a forecast of our day, it is for our day. We need the confidence that the Revelator inspires, that despite the brutal forces of evil in our world, in the long run they do not stand the ghost of a show against the stronger power of God.

"But right is right, since God is God,
     And right the day must win;
   To doubt would be disloyalty,
     To falter would be sin."

XII

THE BATTLE WITH THE BEAST

IT IS VERY EVIDENT THAT IT IS NOT POSSIBLE IN a brief volume to make any elaborate comments on the varied contents of the Book of Revelation. A good one-volume commenttary will prove helpful to the general reader.

DIFFICULT PASSAGES

Space will permit calling attention only to some of the more disputed and difficult passages.

First of all is the long debated question that has to do with the "beast" of the Apocalypse. Who or what is the beast? What is the significance of the mark of the beast? Whom does the figure 666 indicate? It is difficult to get a consistent picture of the beast. In chapter 13, two beasts are mentioned. The first part of the chapter deals with the first beast which rose up out of the sea. In verse 11 the transition is made to the second beast. But in verses 15-18 the reference recurs to the first beast with the number 666.

The emperor who "had the wound by the sword and did live," according to most interpreters, indicates Nero, who, according to a prevalent tradition, came to life again. He was, and is not, and yet is."

It must be kept in mind that there is no prediction of the far future and that all fanciful application of the prophecy to some recent pope or dictator does violence to all sane interpretation. Emphasis must be given to the fact that the author is dealing with his own present and the immediate future.

Who, then, is the first beast? I think commentators are on the wrong trail who attempt to make a definite application. The term is elastic. Reckoning with all of the references, there is doubtless a description of Nero, and a veiled allusion to Domitian, and also to the Roman Empire itself as the persecutor of Christians. The description of the first beast in 13:1-2 fits the idea of the Roman Empire rather than an individual. The beast had "seven heads and ten horns, and upon his horns ten crowns, and upon his heads the name of blasphemy." It was "like unto a leopard," with "the feet of a bear, and his mouth was as the mouth of a lion." But the primary application of the term "beast" does not prevent the writer from applying it to an emperor, since the authority of an

106

institution is concentrated in a man. But there is the primary meaning of the Empire, with the seven heads standing for seven emporers; and the ten horns are ten kings who are subordinate to the emperors.

The term "beast" when it has an individual significance is a true picture of Domitian, the ruling emperor when the Apocalypse was written. The name "blasphemy" in 13:1 is pertinent to Domitian, since he had ordered himself called "Our Lord" and "Our God." Those who refuse to worship the beast must look forward to the death of martyrdom. In the reign of Domitian the Church was subjected to the fiercest persecution, due to the refusal of Christians to worship the emperor.

What is the mark of the beast? The explicit declaration in 20:4 is that the mark of the beast was on the forehead or hand.

Here arises the mooted question as to the number 666. This may be passed over as indeterminate. Interpreters have indulged in much and varied speculation. Some have figured out the three sixes as clearly pointing to Nero, but this has never been made clear. Others have employed the numerical significance of names with the claim that it denotes the Roman Empire, termed Lateinos. The most reasonable explanation appears to be that seven stands for a perfect number; six falls

107

below it into imperfection, and the 666 is the embodiment of evil.

This first beast was doubtless the brutal force of Rome, and likewise applied to the cruel emperors Nero and Domitian. The reference to the beast "whose wound was healed" in 13:13 appears to indicate Nero in line with the tradition that he came back to life. But the demand of emperor worship in 13:15 more fitly describes Domitian, the first emperor who commanded that he should be worshiped.

Notice may be made now of some of the eccentricities of Adventism. The number 666 has direct reference to the Pope of Rome, since the numeral letters of Vicar of the Son of God make up the number. The first beast in chapter 13 is the Roman papacy. The deadly wound of the beast was inflicted by revolutionary France in 1798. The deadly wound was healed in 1929 when the papacy received a renewal of power.

The second beast in 13:11 had two horns like a lamb and spoke like a dragon. This according to Adventism refers to the United States. The two horns of the lamb stand for civil and religious liberty. Who could be so bold as to question such infallible utterances?

One may venture to ask, however, how these writers know that the author of Revelation had in mind a modern nation? How do the humble followers of these leaders know that they speak infallibly? Adventists are strong in their profession of loyalty to the Scripture. In reality these writers pervert the Scriptures by their irrational and strained interpretation.

THE SECOND BEAST AND THE DRAGON

What is the second beast? In 13:11-14 is the description of the second beast that had two horns like a lamb and that emerged from the earth. This beast is the pagan priesthood, the agency of the Empire for enforcing the worship of the emperor. It typified the official religious administration, the special Roman functionaries throughout the Empire.

What is meant by the dragon? In 12:3-4 is the account of the great red dragon having seven heads, and ten horns, and seven crowns upon his heads. His tail drew a third of all the stars of heaven and did cast them to the earth. The description parallels that of the first beast, but has the additional appendage of a tail. It was some tail! The dragon is Satan, the devil, the serpent who waged war in heaven, and the two beasts waged war on earth.

Satan makes use of the Roman Empire, the seven-headed beast, in his antagonism to the Church.

109

The dragon or Satan is the dark and potent agency back of all the evil forces turned loose on earth. "The dragon gives power to the beast." The first beast, which is Rome, or, in some instances, an emperor, is the agent of the dragon; and the second beast, the pagan priesthood, is the agent of the first beast.

THE COMING VICTORY

The note of the victory of the saints sounds forth in chapter 15. In chapter 19 the picture is drawn of the victorious rider of the white horse. "His eyes were as a flame of fire, and on his head were many crowns; and he had a name written, that no one knew but he himself." He wore "a vesture dipped in blood: and his name is called The Word of God."

The armies in heaven followed him upon white horses, clothed in fine linen, white and clean. Out of his mouth goes a sharp sword with which he would smite the nations, and he shall rule them with a rod of iron, and he treads the winepress of the fierceness and wrath of Almighty God. He has on his vesture and on his thigh, a name written "King of Kings, and Lord of Lords."

The triumph is complete. The beast is taken, and "the false prophet that wrought miracles before him, with which he deceived them that bore the mark of the beast, and them that worshiped his image." These both were cast into the lake of fire, burning with brimstone. The shout of the coming victory was of incalculable encouragement to the persecuted Christians. "And I heard as it were the voice of a great multitude, and as the voice of many waters, and as the voice of mighty thunderings, saying, Allelulia; for the Lord God omnipotent reigneth."

Above the strife and confusion of the earth, God the Creator and the Omnipotent reigns, and the triumph of the powers of darkness is only temporary. The beast will be vanquished. Early Christian thought identified Nero with the anti-Christ. Jewish apocalyptists taught that just before the end of the world, a diabolic being would appear who would usurp the place of the Messiah.

THE FORTY-TWO MONTHS

Just here a prophecy of the measure of time of the persecution of Rome before the final victory is found in 11:2-3 and 13:5. What is the explanation of the three and half years, or forty-two months, or 1,260 days? The saints of God were persecuted for forty-two months.

The marvelous mathematics of Adventism on these figures has already received attention in the chapter on Daniel. The chronology of Adventism is entirely imaginary.

We must again remind our readers that the Revelator has to do with his present and immediate future. The forty-two months are taken from Daniel. This was the period of the persecution under Antiochus Epiphanes, 168-165 B.C., and is employed by the author of Revelation to mark the duration of the persecution of the Christians.

Whether this period of time is a qualitative expression and is to be construed as a symbol or as expressing an actual lapse of time, should not be dogmatically decided. It is a forecast of the speedy overthrow of the beast of oppression, and the promise of the coming victory of God and the Messiah and the saints.

It could have been of no avail to the struggling and harassed Church to have prophesied a remote triumph after the lapse of a score of centuries.

In reality the principles of darkness and light have their conflict in every age. We are to battle against the incarnation of secularism and materialism in our day. The embodiment of the pagan ideas of savagery, of cruelty and injustice, continues to make war on the spiritual forces of righteousness.

> "Be strong!
> It matters not how deep entrenched the wrong,
> How hard the battle goes, the day, how long;
> Faint not, fight on! tomorrow comes the song."

XIII

THE THOUSAND YEARS

THE DECLARATION MAY BE SAFELY MADE THAT no other portion of the entire Bible has been the arena of such fierce theological conflicts as the twentieth chapter of the Book of Revelation. This chapter has been and still is the "happy hunting ground" of visionaries and religious fanatics. Many wild fanatical movements have been occasioned by this scriptural passage.

The doctrine of the thousand years physical reign of Christ rests solely on this one reference in a highly figurative book. This passage runs counter to all of the rest of the Bible, yet Adventists attach more authority to it than to all other portions of Scripture. Their whole system rests on the precarious foundation of this one passage. Their method of reading a thousand years reign of Christ into the Scriptures is altogether arbitrary. The number of years of the earthly kingdom is variously estimated in apocalyptic literature. Esdras, an apocryphal book, estimates it at four hundred years.

The author of Revelation sets forth a messianic reign of a thousand years preceding the final judgment. We have already noted that the prevalent apocalyptic literature affords "the key to the mysteries." The first reference to a thousand years is in the Slavonic Book or Enoch, which was written in the first half of the first century. A mere knowledge of the existence of this type of literature affords an explanation of the appearance of the symbols and figures in Revelation. The period of a time, two times, and half a time, or forty-two months, or 1,260 days, represents the duration of the opression of satanic forces. The period of a thousand years symbolizes the victorious reign of the martyrs with Christ.

DIFFERENCE OF INTERPRETATION

There are some three viewpoints of the thousand years. The first, the view of Adventism, construes the passage literally and makes the claim that Christ will reign over a physical kingdom for a thousand years. This is the notion of all Adventist groups despite their variation in other items of doctrine. The millennialists have endeavored to array John Wesley as an advocate of their view. However, in his comments on Acts 1:6 he condemns the idea: "The disciples still seem to dream of an outward temporal Kingdom, in which the Jews should have dominion over all nations." Dr. C. I. Scofield labors long in reading the thousand years into a large number of scriptural passages.

The second theory is that the Revelator had in mind the actual period of a thousand years, but was under the influence of traditional apocalyptic notions. The biblical scholars who advocate this second theory, while not accepting the Adventist doctrine, hold that the author of Revelation did indicate a period of a thousand actual years.

The third view, held by the larger number of biblical scholars, is that the term of a thousand years has a qualitative rather than numerical significance. Satan is completely bound. It is held that the pictorial language concerning the period of time is to be taken as a symbol. A choice between the second and third view is really of no importance. Both views run counter to the literalism of Adventism.

Adventism is out of harmony with orthodoxy. The adherents of the theory are ultraorthodox in their profession, and it may appear rather curious to bring against them the accusation of heresy. The Apostles' Creed has no place for a thousand years visible reign of Christ in the phrase, "From thence he shall come to judge the quick and the dead." There is no premillennial reign in the Nicene Creed. The Augsburg Confession and the Helvetic Confession both condemn the Jewish dreams of the physical reign of Messiah. Neither the Westminster Confession nor the Thirty-nine Articles of the Anglican Church, nor the Twenty-five Articles of The Methodist Church gives any support to this theory.

THE REIGNING SAINTS

In Revelation 20: 4, the reigning saints are those who "were beheaded for the witness of Jesus, and for the word of God, and which had not worshiped the beast, neither his image, neither had received his mark upon their foreheads, or in their hands; and they lived and reigned with Christ for a thousand years." The Adventists make a broad inclusiveness of these words to include all of the righteous dead. They claim that in addition to the martyrs the latter part of the verse includes those who had not worshiped the beast but who had not suffered martyrdom as among the reigning saints. The fact, however, is the number is limited to martyrs. This is made even more explicit in 13:15, since all those who refuse to worship the image of the beast are martyred. So evidently the only possibility of the Adventists being numbered with those who reign with Christ is to suffer martyrdom. In reality, however, this would not include them, since the writer is referring only to the martyrs of his own day.

THE SECOND COMING AND THE JUDGMENT

The doctrine of Adventism is that the righteous dead will be raised at the coming of Christ and that a thousand years afterward the wicked will be raised up and judged. A thousand years will intervene between the two resurrections. In direct opposition to this, the uniform teaching of Scripture is that the final coming of Christ is attended with the general resurrection and judgment. It is not necessary to mention the various references refuting the Adventist notion, which is made plausible only by juggling with words. Take, for example, the quotation from John 5:28, 29: "Marvel not at this: for the hour is coming, in the which all that are in the graves shall hear his voice, and shall come forth; they that have done good, unto the resurrection of life: and they that have done evil, unto the resurrection of damnation." Adventists do violence to this scripture and interpret the "hour" as a thousand years. They prove anything to their own satisfaction by making anything mean anything to suit their purpose.

In the coming of the Son of Man and the final judgment in Matthew, chapter 25, there is no interval between the coming and the judgment. While the Adventists rely mainly on the twentieth chapter of Revelation, yet even this does not support the idea of the interval between the resurrection of the righteous and the wicked. The first resurrection was only of the martyred saints. The Revelator "saw the souls of them that were beheaded." The general judgment in which all the dead, the good and the evil, stood before the throne is in verse 12: "And I saw the dead, small and great, standing before God; and the books were opened: and another book was opened, which is the book of life: and the dead were judged out of those things which were written in the books, according to their works." No intervening period is allowed between the judgment of the righteous and the unrighteous. The Adventists place their special emphasis on Revelation and then misinterpret it.

Aside from questions of exegesis the only reasonable attitude is to recognize that the whole idea of a millennium is a conception derived from the Jewish apocalyptic literature of the first Christian century. It may be re-emphasized that the idea is not found in the teachings of Jesus, or in any other part of the Scriptures. It had its origin in the blending of the passages from Genesis of the seven days of creation, and the expression in the Psalms,

"For a thousand years in thy sight are but as yesterday."

The literalism of the Adventist involves him in insuperable difficulties. He adheres to a literal inerrancy of the Bible. However, he practically denies the inerrancy of all the Scriptures except the Book of Revelation. He then proceeds to deny the accuracy even of this book. The author states that he is writing of "things which must shortly come to pass." "Behold I come quickly." Adventists persist in striking their heads against the facts. Their heads may be hard, but the facts are still harder. By and by something will be broken, and it will not be the facts that are broken.

The closing part of chapter 20 depicts the release of Satan from his prison and the renewal of the conflict. Satan is finally overcome and cast into the lake of fire and brimstone. Chapter 22 pictures the Holy City and the final separation of the good and evil.

A study of Revelation and its purpose, and a freedom from literalists with a diseased imagination, brings to one a new appreciation of the abiding spiritual values of the book.

XIV

THE APOCALYPSE AND SPIRITUAL VALUES

THE LARGER NUMBER OF BIBLE READERS HAVE never entered into a realization of the inestimable values of the books of Daniel and Revelation. As we have already observed this contribution of value of Daniel, we wish to summarize some of the spiritual values of the Book of Revelation.

THE VINDICTIVENESS AND EXPLANATION

Many modern readers are repelled by the fierceness of divine wrath which flames through the pages of Revelation. It is out of harmony with the conception of God as Father which is in the gospels and epistles. The lurid description of the divine vengeance inflicted on the enemies of the Church appears to be contrary to the fatherly love revealed in Christ. The Messiah treads the winepress of the fierceness of God's wrath and smites the nations with a sharp sword and rules them with a rod of

iron. Blood gushes out as high as a horse's bridle for the space of two hundred miles. The birds are summoned to feast on the enemies of the Faith until they are glutted with the flesh of foes.

This bitter intolerance can be understood only as it is seen against the dark background of the cruel persecution which dooms all Christians to death. In his own style the author is saying that the divine judgment against sin is inevitable and severe, and the fact that this retribution was immediate served to bring new courage to the oppressed Christians.

The Adventists lay hold of the stern features of God drawn in the time of a fearful crisis and from it frame their total picture of God. They largely obscure the spiritual values. They have lifted the book out of its historical setting and purpose and have transplanted the symbols with arbitrary mathematical calculations to modern persecutors and nations. We need to reiterate that it would have been of no comfort for these early Christians to be informed of the happenings in the world twenty and more centuries in the future. The author wrote for his readers to understand. The contemporary readers would not have understood if the Revelator were talking about the papacy or modern dictators.

The true interpretation of the book unveils the

unrealized veins of gold that have been hidden by the bizarre fancies of Adventism.

THE LETTERS TO THE SEVEN CHURCHES

The symbolic number seven possibly indicates that the messages were intended for other churches than those named. This much is true: the sins rebuked and the Christian graces commended in the letters to the seven churches and the spiritual reward of the overcoming life are of timeless application. The spiritual lessons are evident—the loss of the fervor of first love of the church of Ephesus, the lukewarmness of the church at Laodicea, and the vices and virtues of the other churches.

SOME THINGS WORTH MORE THAN LIFE

A cowardly neutrality has no place in the Christian life in the battle between the powers of darkness and the powers of light. The call to heroic living sounds throughout the book. "Be thou faithful unto death!"

The Revelator is seeking to inspire courage in the spirits of the persecuted Christians. The Church is not alone in its struggle against the pagan power of Rome, but the omnipotent resources of Heaven are the allies of the Church.

"Thrice blest is he to whom is given
   The instinct that can tell,
That God is in the field
   When he is most invisible."

MORAL LAW INTERWOVEN IN THE WORLD

The long perspective of history confirms the fact that evil does not work well in our world and that moral law is as truly a constituent principle of the universe as the physical law of gravitation. Material forces must at last yield before the supremacy of moral forces. The rise or fall of nations is conditional on obedience to moral law.

The triumph of righteousness and the overthrow of evil are assured by the very nature of the universe in which we live. The stars in their courses fight against the wrong. Right may be for awhile on the scaffold and wrong on the throne, but throughout the Book of Revelation the doom of the dragon is sure and, despite the persistency of evil, the good is marked for ultimate dominion.

As a consequence of the moral order of the world, inevitable judgment is against unrighteousness. This judgment will not take place in the pictorial and spectacular manner, as expressed in apocalyptic style. But the retribution that follows on the heels of evil is no less certain and severe.

123

THE SUPREME ALLEGIANCE

The Book of Revelation has an indispensable value for our modern world in that it declares in no uncertain terms where our ultimate loyalty belongs.

The Church must never surrender its soul to the state. We must recognize that the state has a necessary function and that we owe a duty to the state. The highest service that the Church can give to the state is keeping the consciences of individuals alive to their supreme obligation to God. If an unavoidable conflict arises, nothing is left for the Christian but "to obey God rather than men."

The record of the state has not been such as to entitle it to our blind and unconditional obedience. The political power of the state pressed the cup of poison to the lips of Socrates, crucified Jesus on the cross, and brought Paul to the headman's block.

Jesus recognized the inevitable antagonism. He says, "Ye shall be brought before the governors and kings for my sake." He declared our duty to the state, "Give to Caesar what belongs to Caesar"; but absolute devotion belongs to God, "Give God what belongs to God." Human government is valid only as the expression of the divine will. Jesus answered Pilate, "You would have no power over me, unless it had been granted you from above." The message of Revelation as of Daniel

124

is that there can be but one supreme allegiance, and that allegiance is unto God.

The battle symbolically pictured in Revelation is not simply a conflict between the Church and the Roman Empire. Invisible spiritual forces are engaged. The dragon, or Satan, is the ally of the beast, or Roman Empire.

God himself and the Messiah, the Christ of God, are the allies of the Church. Looking underneath the symbols, these are the opposing forces. It is an unequal contest, for the "Lord God omnipotent reigneth." The author sees all human history molded by the hand of God. He sees God "within the shadow, keeping watch above his own." He is "King of Kings, and Lord of Lords," whose power is far beyond that of the Roman Empire, or of the emperor, a mere puppet, who calls himself "Lord" and "God." He sees the Christ, the rider of the white horse, pictured in the strength of a conqueror.

Over against the despair of human weakness is the faith that there is no indifference on the part of God. The Redeemer and Deliverer will come, and deliverance is on the way. The devil or the dragon is doomed to defeat. "And the devil was cast into the lake of fire."

The author was writing primarily for his own day, but in doing this he brings confidence in the ultimate victory of the good to our day. The victory of the early Christians over paganism is the promise that the Church of today may repeat their victory as we battle against the entrenched forces of materialism and militarism.

The author gives continual emphasis to the fact that our God is a living God. He is in contrast with the lifeless idols of paganism. He is in contrast with the God of present day Humanism, a God who is an abstraction, a mere principle of concretion. Jesus is a living Christ who conquered death and the grave. The living God and the living Christ win through the power of love and self-sacrifice. The victorious rider of the white horse is also the Lamb, "slain from the foundation of the world." The love that is sacrificial, the Cross of Christ, is the strong power that will at last achieve the longed for victory.

We are prone to doubt the overcoming power of this kind of God and of this kind of Christ. He is not a Christ of cruelty, but a Christ whose love and gentleness do not prevent his opposition to the forces of evil. The Revelator draws in poetic language the eternal truth that Satan in his strength is no match for God. Sovereignty belongs to God, and he overrules all events to the consummation of his purpose. We cannot hold the author to absolute accuracy as touching some predictive elements, as for example the immediate downfall of the Roman Empire. But his prediction is entirely true that spiritual forces are sure to win. A true understanding makes it a book for our day. We could ill afford to be without the Book of Revelation. We are in need of the constant refrain of hope and heroism which the book inspires.

The exercise of this power of love brought victory to the early Church. This power of a living, loving God will win the battle of Armageddon, the final conflict of the Apocalypse. We are prone to discouragement over the physical might of a godless totalitarianism and a brutal militarism. But in the long run these evil forces do not stand the shadow of a show against the almightiness of the Almighty God.

The Book of Revelation has an urgent and needed message for our modern world. The beast of secularism is embodied in men and institutions and carries on the persistent antagonism against the spiritual forces that make for righteousness and peace. Ultimate victory is made certain by the moral order of the world and by the omnipotence of God.

> "And when the strife is fierce, the warfare long
> Steals on the ear the distant triumph song,
> And hearts are brave again, and arms are strong."

APPENDIX—A SUMMARY

THE VARIOUS GROUPS OF ADVENTISTS CONTAIN some devout and sincere people. This realization does not remove the necessity of combating the errors.

1. Premillennialism preaches a hopeless gospel. It may be said in reply that it looks forward to the victorious millennial reign of Christ. But a hope of victory based on a false expectation of methods that will never be employed is the equivalent of pessimism.

2. The influence of Adventism on the life of the Church has never been conducive to normal Christian activities and has led to strife and dissension. It results in unbalancing the mind and has often culminated in insanity.

3. Adventism clings to a notion which history has continually refuted. More than nineteen centuries of error in prediction cannot make a fact. Adventists refuse to learn from the lessons of the past. Through all of the Christian centuries they have lived in the "last days." They have become

more wary of date fixing. However, in their fore-cast of the immediacy of the second coming, they practically fix a date. This is especially true in time of war and calamity.

4. The Adventists have no knowledge of the whole body of apocalyptic literature. As a conse-quence, they fall into an utterly irrational inter-pretation of the books of Daniel and Revelation. These are their favorite books, which they totally misunderstand.

5. Adventists develop angularities and peculiar-ities which interfere with their helpful co-opera-tion in the Church.

6. Adventists fall into a kind of self-righteous-ness. This results from dwelling on the wickedness and hopelessness of the world. They remind one of the old brother who always sang in a key above the others and changed the preposition in the familiar hymn:

"Sweet prospects, sweet birds, and sweet flowers,
  Have all lost their sweetness but me."

7. Some good people who hold to the doctrine of Adventism are the victims of a method which in-dulges in sophistry. They bend the Scriptures from their true meaning to fit their eccentric notions.

8. This entire group are too cocksure of an in-sight into the "secret councils of the Almighty."

9. They are Fundamentalists who miss the fundamentals and stress the incidentals. They may be termed more correctly the incidentalists.

10. Their strained interpretation obscures the clear meaning of the Scriptures.

11. They pursue the mode of the crudest literalism. But when this is not in accord with their theory, they turn to the fanciful and allegorical.

12. They refuse to change or to enlarge their conception of God. They close their minds against both biblical scholarship and scientific knowledge. They are illustrations of an arrested mental development. To endeavor to put over this doctrine on our educated young people would tend to produce infidelity.

13. Adventism is in bondage to the sensational and places its confidence solely in the spectacular. It misinterprets the highly figurative language of the Eastern people.

14. Adventism is a reversal to obsolete religious conceptions, and is two-thirds Judaic in its belief in the restoration of Jewish ceremonial sacrifices and nationalism.

15. Where consistently held, Adventism cuts the nerve of all striving for social betterment and world peace. The great social and spiritual mission of the prophets is largely ignored.

16. Adventists hold to a false conception of the

message of the prophets. They project their message, written primarily by the prophets for their own day, into a far distant future. They interpret prophecy as history written in advance.

17. Adventism constructs its superstructure of belief on isolated proof texts and disconnected passages. It bases its doctrine mainly on the precarious foundation of one passage concerning the millennium.

18. The most sacrilegious feature of Adventism is in transforming the compassionate Christ into a cruel military leader.

19. The Adventism of the various groups is a heresy since it is contrary to the historic creeds of the Church, and is out of harmony with the main trend of the Scriptures. Adventists, however, fasten the labels of modernism and infidelity on all who do not pronounce their shibboleth.

20. The notions of Adventists are completely out of harmony with the rich and varied contents of the Kingdom of God. They discount the spiritual nature and gradual growth of the Kingdom.

21. Adventism holds to the verbal dictation theory of inspiration and to the dead-level idea of revelation. This results in un-Christian ethical ideals, and is a denial of the supreme authority of Jesus, who declared, "It has been said to you by them of old . . . . but I say unto you."

22. Adventists deal in a fantastic and fanciful manner with symbols and numbers. The chart which they draw of the future is a marvelous map of misinformation. The projection of minute details of prophecy into a remote future is a violation of all true interpretation.

23. Adventists falsely identify the second coming of Christ which pervades the Scriptures with their idea of a material millennial kingdom.

24. Adventism is a system of fatalism, since the human factor and co-operation with God in establishing the Kingdom is reduced to the vanishing point.

25. As to some doctrines about which there is a difference of opinion, I am not positive. But I am positively certain that Adventism is wrong and is contrary to both reason and revelation.

BIBLIOGRAPHY

ALLEN, C. H. *The Message of the Book of Revelation.* Nashville: Cokesbury Press, 1939.

BERRY, G. R. *Premillennialism and Old Testament Prediction.* Chicago: University of Chicago Press, 1929.

CALKINS, RAYMOND. *The Social Message of the Book of Revelation.* New York: The Womans Press, 1920.

CLARK, ELMER T. *The Small Sects in America.* Nashville: Cokesbury Press, 1938.

GORE, CHARLES. *A New Commentary on the Holy Scripture.* New York: The Macmillan Company, 1928.

HASTINGS, JAMES. *Dictionary of the Apostolic Church.* New York: Charles Scribner's Sons, 1916.

————. *Dictionary of the Bible.* New York: Charles Scribner's Sons, 1920.

HEFFERN, ANDREW D. *Apology and Polemic in the New Testament.* New York: The Macmillan Company, 1922.

HOPWOOD, P. G. S. *The Religious Experience of the Primitive Church.* Edinburgh: T. and T. Clark, 1936.

MOULTON, RICHARD G. *The Modern Reader's Bible for Schools.* New York: The Macmillan Company, 1922.

PARSONS, ERNEST WILLIAM. *The Religion of the New Testament.* New York: Harper and Brothers, 1939.

PEAKE, ARTHUR S. *The Revelation of John.* London: Holborn Publishing House, 1922.

RALL, HARRIS FRANKLIN. *Modern Premillennialism and the Christian Hope.* New York: The Abingdon Press, 1920.

RUSSELL, DANIEL. *Preaching the Apocalypse.* New York: The Abingdon Press, 1935.

SCOTT, E. F. *The Book of Revelation.* New York: Charles Scribner's Sons, 1940.

SCOTT, E. F. *The Kingdom of God in the New Testament.* New York: The Macmillan Company, 1931.

SHELDON, HENRY C. *Studies in Recent Adventism.* New York: The Abingdon Press, 1915.

SMITH, GEORGE ADAM. *The Book of Twelve Prophets.* New York: Doubleday, Doran and Company, 1929.

SNOWDEN, JAMES H. *The Coming of the Lord.* New York: The Macmillan Company, 1921.

STEVENS, GEORGE BARKER. *The Theology of the New Testament.* New York: Charles Scribner's Sons, 1899.

WISHART, C. F. *The Book of Day, and Studies in the Revelation of St. John.* New York: Charles Scribner's Sons, 1935.

The Abingdon Bible Commentary. New York: The Abingdon Press, 1929.

Church and State in the Modern World—A Symposium. New York: Harper and Brothers, 1938.

The Encyclopedia Americana. New York: Americana Corporation, 1939.

The New International Encyclopedia. New York: Dodd, Mead and Company, 1910.